An Ultimate User Guide for Mastering

OnePlus 12

A Comprehensive and In-Depth Practical Guide with Tips and Trick to Maximizing Your Use to Unlocking the Full Potential of your device

Eugene J. Kelly

Dedication

To the unwavering support and boundless love of my parents who have been the steadfast pillars upon which my dreams have soared. Your encouragement and belief in my journey have been the driving force behind every word penned in this book.

To my well-wishers, whose optimism and cheering voices have echoed in the background of my writing days, providing the motivation needed to overcome challenges and embrace triumphs. Your belief in my creative endeavors has been a source of inspiration that I carry with pride.

And, above all, to the Almighty, the Divine orchestrator of destinies, who granted me the gift of creativity and the opportunity to weave stories. In moments of solitude and uncertainty, your guidance has been my compass, steering me through the labyrinth of imagination.

May the words within these pages be a humble offering of gratitude to those whose love and blessings have illuminated my path. This book is dedicated to the enduring spirits of family, friendship, and the Divine forces that shape our narratives.

Table of Contents

Chapter Thirteen: Troubleshooting and FAQs 336

Conclusion 355

Appendices 362

Introduction to OnePlus 12

Overview of OnePlus as a Brand

OnePlus has solidified its place in the smartphone industry as a disruptive force, challenging established players with its innovative approach to design, performance, and user experience. Founded in December 2013, OnePlus quickly gained attention by offering flagship-level smartphones at more affordable prices, earning a dedicated fan base known as the "OnePlus community."

At the heart of OnePlus's philosophy is a commitment to delivering a "Never Settle" experience, a mantra that drives the company to constantly push the boundaries of technology and design. This ethos is reflected in every aspect of their products, from hardware specifications to software features, all aimed at providing users with a premium experience without the premium price tag.

Over the years, OnePlus has garnered praise for its focus on user feedback and community engagement, often incorporating suggestions and ideas directly from its users into its products. This collaborative approach has helped OnePlus cultivate a loyal following and establish itself as a brand that listens to its customers.

With each new release, OnePlus aims to raise the bar for what users can expect from a smartphone, introducing cutting-edge features and technologies while maintaining a commitment to simplicity and elegance in design. From the sleek and minimalist aesthetics to the powerful performance and intuitive user interface, OnePlus devices embody the company's vision of "burdenless" technology that seamlessly integrates into users' lives.

As OnePlus continues to evolve and expand its product lineup, the OnePlus 12 represents the culmination of years of innovation and refinement, promising to deliver an unparalleled smartphone experience that stays true to the brand's core values of performance, quality, and user-centric design.

Evolution of OnePlus Phones

Since its inception, OnePlus has been at the forefront of innovation in the smartphone industry, consistently pushing boundaries and redefining what users expect from their mobile devices. The evolution of OnePlus phones showcases a journey marked by groundbreaking features, design advancements, and a commitment to delivering top-tier performance at competitive prices.

OnePlus One (2014): The OnePlus One marked the company's debut in the smartphone market, offering flagship-level specifications at a fraction of the cost. With its powerful Snapdragon 801 processor, 5.5-inch Full HD display, and customizable CyanogenMod software, the OnePlus One garnered widespread acclaim for its exceptional value for money.

OnePlus 2 (2015): Building on the success of its predecessor, the OnePlus 2 introduced several key upgrades, including a faster Snapdragon 810 processor, a fingerprint sensor, and USB Type-C connectivity. The device also featured OnePlus's proprietary OxygenOS, offering a clean and customizable user experience.

OnePlus 3 (2016): The OnePlus 3 represented a significant leap forward in terms of design and performance. With its sleek metal unibody construction, Snapdragon 820 processor, and 6GB of RAM, the OnePlus 3 delivered flagship-level performance in a premium package. The introduction of Dash Charge technology also set a new standard for fast charging in smartphones.

OnePlus 5 (2017): The OnePlus 5 continued the company's tradition of offering high-end specifications at an affordable price point. Key highlights included the dual-camera setup, featuring a primary 16MP sensor and a secondary 20MP telephoto lens, as well as the Snapdragon 835 processor and up to 8GB of RAM.

OnePlus 6 (2018): With the OnePlus 6, the company focused on refining its design language and introducing new features. The device featured a glass back design, a larger 6.28-inch display with a notch, and improved cameras with enhanced low-light performance. The OnePlus 6 also introduced water resistance for the first time in the company's lineup.

OnePlus 7 (2019): The OnePlus 7 series comprised the OnePlus 7 and OnePlus 7 Pro, catering to different segments of the market. The OnePlus 7 Pro, in particular, stood out with its 90Hz Fluid AMOLED display, pop-up selfie camera, and triple-camera setup, including a 48MP primary sensor.

OnePlus 8 (2020): The OnePlus 8 series introduced 5G connectivity across the lineup, along with the Snapdragon 865 processor and up to 12GB of RAM. The OnePlus 8 Pro featured a quad-camera setup with advanced imaging capabilities, including a 48MP primary sensor and a 48MP ultra-wide sensor with a unique color filter lens.

OnePlus 9 (2021): Collaborating with Hasselblad, the OnePlus 9 series focused on elevating the smartphone photography experience. The OnePlus 9 Pro, in particular, featured a Hasselblad-tuned camera system, delivering stunning image quality and enhanced color accuracy. The series also introduced Warp Charge 65T for blazing-fast charging speeds.

OnePlus 12 (TBD): The OnePlus 12 represents the latest chapter in the company's journey of innovation and excellence. Expected to build upon the foundation laid by its predecessors, the OnePlus 12 is anticipated to feature cutting-edge technologies, refined design, and a host of new features aimed at delivering an unparalleled smartphone experience.

Anticipation and Expectations for OnePlus 12

As OnePlus enthusiasts eagerly await the release of the OnePlus 12, anticipation is at an all-time high, fueled by rumors, leaks, and speculation surrounding the upcoming device. With each new iteration, OnePlus raises the bar for what users can expect from a smartphone, and the OnePlus 12 is no exception. Here's a look at some of the key areas where fans and industry observers are anticipating significant improvements and innovations:

Design and Build Quality: OnePlus has always been praised for its sleek and premium designs, and the OnePlus 12 is expected to continue this trend. Anticipated design elements include a refined form factor, possibly with slimmer bezels and a more ergonomic feel. Whether OnePlus opts for a glass or metal construction, users can expect attention to detail and craftsmanship that exude sophistication.

Display Technology: The display has always been a highlight of OnePlus devices, offering vibrant colors, smooth responsiveness, and immersive viewing experiences. For the OnePlus 12, expectations are high for advancements in display technology, including higher refresh rates, improved brightness levels, and possibly even new display materials or form factors to enhance visual quality and user experience.

Performance and Hardware: OnePlus smartphones are known for their blazing-fast performance, thanks to top-of-the-line processors, ample RAM, and optimized software. With the OnePlus 12, users can anticipate even greater performance capabilities, possibly with the latest Snapdragon chipset, increased RAM options, and optimizations to enhance multitasking, gaming, and overall responsiveness.

Camera System: Smartphone photography has become increasingly important, and OnePlus has been steadily improving its camera offerings with each new release. For the OnePlus 12, expectations are high for further enhancements to camera hardware, such as higher megapixel counts, larger sensors, and innovative camera features. Collaboration with imaging partners, similar to the Hasselblad partnership on the OnePlus 9 series, could also elevate the OnePlus 12's camera capabilities to new heights.

Battery Life and Charging: With users demanding longer battery life and faster charging speeds, OnePlus has been focused on delivering solutions that address these needs. The OnePlus 12 is anticipated to feature advancements in battery technology, potentially offering larger battery capacities or more efficient power management. Additionally, users can expect continued improvements in charging speeds, with OnePlus likely introducing faster charging technologies to minimize downtime and keep users connected throughout the day.

Software Experience: OxygenOS, OnePlus's custom Android skin, has long been praised for its clean design, smooth performance, and useful features. For the OnePlus 12, users can expect further refinements to OxygenOS, with optimizations to improve efficiency, enhance customization options, and introduce new software features that enhance productivity, security, and overall user experience.

Overall, the anticipation and expectations for the OnePlus 12 are driven by a desire for innovation, excellence, and a commitment to delivering a smartphone experience that exceeds expectations. With its track record of pushing boundaries and listening to user feedback, OnePlus is poised to once again raise the bar for what users can expect from their smartphones with the OnePlus 12.

Chapter One: Unboxing and Initial Setup

Unboxing Experience

The unboxing experience of a smartphone sets the tone for the entire user journey, providing the first glimpse into the device and its accessories. OnePlus has consistently delivered a premium unboxing experience with its smartphones, and the OnePlus 12 is expected to be no exception.

Packaging Design: The OnePlus 12 is anticipated to come in a sleek and minimalist packaging design, reflecting the company's ethos of simplicity and elegance.

The box itself may feature the iconic OnePlus logo and branding, with clean lines and a premium feel.

Contents of the Box: Upon opening the box, users can expect to find the OnePlus 12 smartphone prominently displayed at the top, nestled securely within a protective tray or sleeve. Beneath the device, users will likely find a compartment containing the included accessories, such as charging cables, power adapters, and possibly additional items like headphones or a protective case.

Attention to Detail: OnePlus pays close attention to detail in its packaging, ensuring that every component is carefully arranged and presented to create a memorable unboxing experience. From the way the accessories are neatly organized to the materials used in the packaging itself, every aspect is thoughtfully designed to evoke a sense of quality and craftsmanship.

Inclusion of Extras: In addition to the essentials like charging cables and adapters, OnePlus often includes extras or surprises in its packaging to delight users. This could include special edition accessories, exclusive offers, or even handwritten notes from the

OnePlus team, further enhancing the unboxing experience and fostering a sense of connection with the brand.

Unveiling the Device: As users lift the OnePlus 12 out of the box for the first time, they are greeted with the stunning design and craftsmanship of the device. Whether it's the sleek curves, premium materials, or striking color options, the OnePlus 12 is sure to make a strong first impression, setting the stage for an exceptional user experience.

The unboxing experience of the OnePlus 12 is expected to be a memorable and enjoyable moment for users, reflecting

OnePlus's commitment to delivering a premium and user-centric smartphone experience from the very first interaction.

Contents of the Box

When you unbox your OnePlus 12, you'll find a carefully curated selection of accessories designed to enhance your experience and provide everything you need to get started right away. OnePlus takes pride in delivering a comprehensive package that covers all the essentials and more, ensuring that users have everything they need to make the most of their new device.

OnePlus 12 Smartphone: The centerpiece of the unboxing

experience is, of course, the OnePlus 12 smartphone itself. Featuring a sleek and sophisticated design, powerful internals, and a host of innovative features, the OnePlus 12 is ready to impress from the moment you lay eyes on it.

Charging Cable: Included in the box is a high-quality charging cable that allows you to power up your OnePlus 12 quickly and conveniently. Whether you prefer the traditional USB Type-A to Type-C cable or the newer USB Type-C to Type-C cable for faster charging speeds, OnePlus has you covered.

Power Adapter: Accompanying the charging cable is a power adapter that provides the necessary juice to keep your OnePlus 12 running smoothly throughout the day. With OnePlus's industry-leading charging technology, you can expect fast and efficient charging times that minimize downtime and keep you connected when you need it most.

Documentation and SIM Tool: OnePlus includes a set of documentation with your OnePlus 12, including a quick start guide, warranty information, and safety instructions to help you get acquainted with your new device.

Additionally, you'll find a handy SIM ejector tool that makes it easy to install your SIM card and get connected to your mobile network.

Protective Case (Possibly): Depending on the region or specific bundle you purchase, OnePlus may include a protective case in the box to help safeguard your OnePlus 12 against bumps, scratches, and other everyday wear and tear. These cases come in a variety of styles and materials, allowing you to choose the one that best suits your preferences and lifestyle.

Additional Accessories (Possibly): In some cases, OnePlus may include additional accessories in the box to enhance your user experience further. This could include items like headphones, screen protectors, or special edition accessories designed in collaboration with partners or artists. These extras add an extra layer of value and excitement to the unboxing experience, making it even more enjoyable for users.

The contents of the OnePlus 12 box are thoughtfully curated to provide everything you need to start using your new smartphone right away. From the essentials like the smartphone itself and charging accessories to additional extras that enhance your experience,

OnePlus ensures that every aspect of the unboxing experience is tailored to delight and impress users.

Initial Setup Process

Once you've unboxed your OnePlus 12 and familiarized yourself with the contents of the box, it's time to dive into the initial setup process. OnePlus strives to make this process as seamless and intuitive as possible, guiding users through the necessary steps to get their device up and running quickly.

Powering On the Device: The first step in the initial setup process is to power on your OnePlus 12. Simply press and hold the power button located on the side or top of the device until you see the OnePlus logo appear on the screen. Once the device powers on, you'll be greeted with the initial setup wizard to guide you through the rest of the process.

Selecting Language and Region: The setup wizard will prompt you to select your preferred language and region. Choose the language that you're most comfortable with and the region that corresponds to your location to ensure that your OnePlus 12 is set up correctly.

Connecting to Wi-Fi or Mobile Network: Next, you'll need to connect your OnePlus 12 to a Wi-Fi network or mobile network to access the internet and download updates. Select your preferred network from the list of available options and enter the password if prompted. If you're setting up a mobile data connection, you may need to insert your SIM card at this stage.

Signing in to Your Google Account: To access Google services and download apps from the Play Store, you'll need to sign in to your Google account. If you don't have a Google account yet, you can create one during the setup process. Once you've signed in or created your account, you'll have the option to restore your data from a previous device if desired.

Setting Up Security Features: OnePlus offers a range of security features to protect your device and personal information. During the initial setup process, you'll have the opportunity to set up features like fingerprint recognition, facial recognition, or a PIN or password to secure your device and keep your data safe.

Customizing Settings and Preferences: As you progress through the setup wizard, you'll have the chance to customize various settings and preferences to suit your preferences. This includes options like display brightness, sound settings, notification preferences, and more. Take the time to adjust these settings according to your preferences to personalize your OnePlus 12 experience.

Completing Setup and Exploring Your Device: Once you've completed the initial setup process, you're ready to start using your OnePlus 12! Take some time to explore the device and familiarize yourself with its features, apps, and capabilities. Whether you're checking out the camera, browsing the web, or downloading your favorite apps from the Play Store, the OnePlus 12 offers a wealth of possibilities to explore and enjoy.

By following these steps, you can quickly and easily set up your OnePlus 12 and start enjoying all that this powerful smartphone has to offer. With its intuitive setup process and user-friendly interface, OnePlus makes it easy for users to get the most out of their device from the very beginning.

Chapter Two: Design and Build Quality

Exterior Design Elements

The design of a smartphone plays a crucial role in its overall appeal and user experience. OnePlus has consistently been praised for its attention to detail and commitment to delivering sleek and stylish designs that not only look great but also feel comfortable in the hand. With the OnePlus 12, users can expect a continuation of this tradition, with a focus on refinement, innovation, and premium materials.

Sleek and Minimalist Aesthetics: OnePlus is known for its

minimalist design philosophy, favoring clean lines, subtle curves, and understated elegance. The OnePlus 12 is expected to embody this aesthetic, with a sleek and streamlined silhouette that exudes sophistication. From the slim profile to the carefully crafted contours, every aspect of the OnePlus 12's design is thoughtfully considered to create a visually striking device that stands out from the crowd.

Premium Materials: OnePlus has a history of using premium materials in its smartphone construction, and the OnePlus 12 is likely to continue this trend.

Whether it's aerospace-grade aluminum, durable glass, or other high-quality materials, users can expect the OnePlus 12 to feel solid and well-built in the hand. The choice of materials not only enhances the device's aesthetic appeal but also contributes to its overall durability and longevity.

Attention to Detail: OnePlus is renowned for its meticulous attention to detail, and this is evident in every aspect of the OnePlus 12's design. From the precision-machined edges to the finely textured finishes, every element is carefully crafted to create a cohesive and harmonious design language. Even small details like the placement of buttons, the symmetry of the camera module, and the alignment of logos are thoughtfully considered to enhance the user experience and create a sense of refinement.

Innovative Features: In addition to its timeless design principles, OnePlus is also known for its innovative approach to smartphone design. With the OnePlus 12, users can expect to see the introduction of new and innovative features that push the boundaries of what's possible in a smartphone. Whether it's a groundbreaking new display technology, a revolutionary camera system, or innovative ways to interact with the device, the OnePlus 12 is sure to offer plenty of surprises and delights for users. Ergonomics and Comfort: Beyond just looks, OnePlus places a strong emphasis on ergonomics and comfort in its device designs. The OnePlus 12 is expected to feature carefully sculpted contours and ergonomic curves that fit comfortably in the hand, making it easy to use for extended periods without fatigue. Attention is also paid to factors like button placement and tactile feedback to ensure a satisfying and intuitive user experience.

The exterior design elements of the OnePlus 12 are poised to set a new standard for smartphone aesthetics, combining sleek and minimalist aesthetics with premium materials, meticulous attention to detail, and innovative features. Whether you're admiring its design from afar or holding it in your hand, the OnePlus 12 is sure to impress with its impeccable craftsmanship and timeless appeal.

Material Quality

One of the defining characteristics of OnePlus smartphones is their commitment to using premium materials that not only enhance the device's aesthetics but also contribute to its durability and overall user experience. With the OnePlus 12, users can expect a continuation of this tradition, with careful attention paid to the selection and implementation of high-quality materials throughout the device's construction.

Aerospace-Grade Aluminum: OnePlus has frequently utilized aerospace-grade aluminum in the construction of its smartphones, and the OnePlus 12 is expected to be no exception. Known for its lightweight yet durable properties, aluminum provides a sturdy foundation for the device while also offering a premium look and feel. The use of aluminum also allows for precise machining and detailing, ensuring that every aspect of the device's design is executed to perfection.

Corning Gorilla Glass: Glass has become a staple material in smartphone design, offering a sleek and premium aesthetic while also providing protection for the device's display. The OnePlus 12 is likely to feature Corning Gorilla Glass, a highly durable and scratch-resistant glass that helps safeguard the device against everyday wear and tear. Whether it's the front display or the rear panel, Gorilla Glass adds an extra layer of protection and refinement to the OnePlus 12's design.

Premium Ceramic: In addition to aluminum and glass, OnePlus has also experimented with premium ceramic materials in its smartphone designs. Ceramic offers a unique blend of strength, scratch resistance, and thermal conductivity, making it an attractive choice for smartphone construction. While not confirmed, there's speculation that the OnePlus 12 may incorporate ceramic elements in its design, further enhancing its durability and premium appeal.

Textured Finishes: Beyond just the choice of materials, OnePlus pays attention to the finer details of surface finishes and textures to enhance the device's tactile feel and grip. Whether it's a matte finish that minimizes fingerprints and smudges or a textured surface that provides added grip and comfort, OnePlus explores a variety of finishing techniques to optimize the user experience.

Environmental Considerations: In addition to prioritizing quality and durability, OnePlus also considers the environmental impact of its material choices. The company is committed to using sustainable and eco-friendly materials whenever possible, minimizing waste and reducing its carbon footprint. This commitment to sustainability ensures that the OnePlus 12 not only looks and feels great but also aligns with the company's values of responsible manufacturing and environmental stewardship.

The material quality of the OnePlus 12 reflects the company's dedication to craftsmanship, innovation, and sustainability. By carefully selecting premium materials and refining their implementation through precision engineering and detailing, OnePlus creates smartphones that not only look and feel premium but also stand the test of time, delivering a superior user experience for years to come.

Ergonomics and Handling

The ergonomic design of a smartphone plays a crucial role in its usability and comfort during everyday use. OnePlus prioritizes ergonomics and handling in the design of its smartphones, ensuring that users can comfortably hold and operate their devices for extended periods without experiencing fatigue or discomfort. With the OnePlus 12, users can expect a continuation of this focus on ergonomics, with careful attention paid to the device's form factor, weight distribution, and physical dimensions.

Slim Profile and Lightweight Construction: OnePlus devices, including the OnePlus 12, typically feature a slim and lightweight construction that makes them easy to hold and carry. The device's slim profile not only enhances its aesthetic appeal but also contributes to a more comfortable grip, allowing users to securely hold the device in one hand without straining their fingers or palm. Additionally, the use of lightweight materials like aluminum and glass helps to minimize the overall weight of the device, further enhancing its portability and ease of handling.

Curved Edges and Contoured Surfaces: OnePlus pays careful attention to the curvature of the device's edges and the contours of its surfaces to ensure a comfortable and ergonomic grip. The OnePlus 12 is likely to feature gently curved edges that fit naturally in the palm of the hand, reducing pressure points and improving overall comfort during prolonged use. Similarly, the device's back panel may feature subtle contours that conform to the shape of the user's hand, providing a secure and ergonomic grip that minimizes the risk of accidental slips or drops.

Optimized Button Placement: The placement and design of physical buttons on the OnePlus 12 are carefully considered to enhance ease of use and accessibility. OnePlus typically positions the power and volume buttons within easy reach of the user's thumb or index finger, allowing for intuitive operation without having to adjust the grip or strain to reach the controls. Additionally, the tactile feedback of the buttons is finely tuned to provide a satisfying click and response, further enhancing the user experience.

Balanced Weight Distribution: A well-balanced weight distribution is essential for comfortable handling and usability, particularly during one-handed operation. OnePlus engineers meticulously distribute the weight of the OnePlus 12 to ensure that it feels balanced and stable in the hand, regardless of how the device is held or oriented. This balanced weight distribution reduces strain on the user's hand and wrist, making it easier to hold the device for extended periods without fatigue.

Optimized Screen-to-Body Ratio: The screen-to-body ratio of the OnePlus 12 is likely to be optimized to maximize the usable screen real estate while minimizing the overall footprint of the device. A high screen-to-body ratio ensures that the device remains compact and easy to handle, despite featuring a large display. This design approach allows users to enjoy immersive multimedia experiences and productivity tasks without compromising on comfort or ergonomics.

The OnePlus 12 is expected to offer a comfortable and ergonomic user experience, with a slim and lightweight design, curved edges, optimized button placement, balanced weight distribution, and an optimized screen-to-body ratio.

By prioritizing ergonomics and handling in the design process, OnePlus ensures that users can enjoy using their devices comfortably and confidently in any situation.

Chapter Three: Display Technology

Screen Size and Resolution

The display is one of the most critical components of a smartphone, serving as the primary interface for interacting with the device and consuming content. OnePlus has a history of equipping its smartphones with high-quality displays that offer vibrant colors, crisp detail, and smooth responsiveness. With the OnePlus 12, users can expect the latest advancements in display technology to deliver an exceptional viewing experience.

Generous Screen Size: The OnePlus 12 is anticipated to feature a generous screen size that strikes a balance between immersive viewing and comfortable handling. While the exact dimensions have not been confirmed, OnePlus typically opts for displays in the range of 6.5 to 6.8 inches, providing ample screen real estate for gaming, multimedia consumption, and productivity tasks without feeling unwieldy or oversized.

High Resolution: To ensure crisp detail and clarity, the OnePlus 12 is expected to boast a high-resolution display with a pixel density of at least 400 pixels per inch (PPI). This ensures that text, images, and graphics appear sharp and well-defined, making for an immersive and enjoyable viewing experience. Whether you're scrolling through social media, reading articles, or watching videos, the high resolution of the OnePlus 12's display ensures that every detail is rendered with precision and accuracy.

Dynamic AMOLED Technology: OnePlus has embraced AMOLED display technology in its recent smartphone releases, and the OnePlus 12 is likely to continue this trend. AMOLED displays offer several advantages over traditional LCD panels, including deeper blacks, higher contrast ratios, and more vibrant colors. With a Dynamic AMOLED display, users can expect rich, true-to-life colors, excellent visibility in various lighting conditions, and an overall stunning visual experience.

High Refresh Rate: OnePlus has been a pioneer in the adoption of high refresh rate displays, offering smoother and more responsive performance compared to standard 60Hz panels. The OnePlus 12 is expected to feature a high refresh rate display, possibly 120Hz or higher, to deliver silky-smooth animations, fluid scrolling, and reduced motion blur during gaming and other fast-paced activities. The higher refresh rate not only enhances the user experience but also contributes to overall device responsiveness and fluidity.

HDR10+ Support: For an enhanced multimedia experience, the OnePlus 12 may offer support for HDR10+ content playback. HDR10+ technology allows for greater dynamic range and color accuracy in supported content, resulting in more lifelike and immersive visuals. Whether you're streaming HDR content from services like Netflix or Amazon Prime Video or viewing HDR-compatible photos and videos, the OnePlus 12's display ensures that you enjoy stunning visuals with exceptional detail and realism.

Overall, the display technology of the OnePlus 12 is poised to deliver an exceptional viewing experience, with a generous screen size, high resolution, Dynamic AMOLED technology, high refresh rate, and HDR10+ support. Whether you're gaming, streaming, or simply browsing the web, the OnePlus 12's display promises to immerse you in stunning visuals that captivate and delight.

Display Panel Type

The display panel type of a smartphone plays a significant role in determining its visual characteristics, including color reproduction, viewing angles, and power efficiency. OnePlus has consistently utilized advanced display panel technologies to deliver immersive and vibrant viewing experiences across its smartphone lineup. With the OnePlus 12, users can expect the continuation of this commitment to display excellence, with the selection of a cutting-edge display panel type.

Dynamic AMOLED Panel: OnePlus smartphones have embraced AMOLED (Active Matrix Organic Light Emitting Diode) display technology in recent iterations, and the OnePlus 12 is likely to feature a Dynamic AMOLED panel. Dynamic AMOLED panels offer several advantages over traditional LCD displays, including deeper blacks, higher contrast ratios, and more vibrant colors. This results in a visually stunning and immersive viewing experience, with lifelike colors and excellent visibility even in bright outdoor conditions.

Benefits of AMOLED Technology:

- Vibrant Colors: AMOLED displays produce colors by emitting light directly from individual pixels, resulting in vibrant and saturated colors that pop off the screen. Whether you're viewing photos, videos, or games, the colors on the OnePlus 12's display are sure to impress with their richness and depth.

- Infinite Contrast Ratio: Unlike LCD displays, which rely on a backlight to illuminate the entire screen, AMOLED panels can individually control each pixel's brightness. This allows for true blacks and an infinite contrast ratio, enhancing the depth and realism of images and videos.

- Fast Response Times: AMOLED displays have faster response times compared to traditional LCD panels, resulting in smoother animations, reduced motion blur, and improved gaming performance. Whether you're scrolling through social media feeds or playing graphically intensive games, the OnePlus 12's display responds quickly and accurately to your touch inputs.

- Energy Efficiency: AMOLED displays are more energy-efficient than LCD panels, as they only consume power when pixels are illuminated. This helps to extend the OnePlus 12's battery life, allowing you to enjoy your favorite content for longer periods without needing to recharge.

Advanced Pixel Arrangement: OnePlus may utilize advanced pixel arrangements, such as PenTile or Diamond PenTile, to further enhance the display's visual fidelity and efficiency. These pixel layouts optimize subpixel arrangements to improve sharpness, reduce pixelation, and minimize power consumption, resulting in a superior viewing experience on the OnePlus 12's display.

Customizable Display Settings: OnePlus devices typically offer a range of customizable display settings, allowing users to adjust color temperature, saturation levels, and screen calibration to suit their preferences. Whether you prefer vibrant and punchy colors or more natural and accurate tones, the OnePlus 12's display settings can be fine-tuned to match your personal preferences and viewing conditions.

Overall, the display panel type of the OnePlus 12 is expected to be a Dynamic AMOLED panel, offering vibrant colors, infinite contrast ratios, fast response times, and energy efficiency. Combined with advanced pixel arrangements and customizable display settings, the OnePlus 12's display promises to deliver a visually stunning and immersive viewing experience that sets a new standard for smartphone displays.

Refresh Rate and HDR Support

The refresh rate and HDR (High Dynamic Range) support are two key aspects of display technology that significantly impact the visual experience on a smartphone. OnePlus has been at the forefront of incorporating high refresh rate displays and HDR support in its devices to deliver smoother visuals and more immersive content consumption experiences. With the OnePlus 12, users can expect these features to be further optimized to enhance the overall viewing experience.

High Refresh Rate: OnePlus smartphones are known for their high refresh rate displays, which offer smoother animations, reduced motion blur, and improved responsiveness compared to traditional 60Hz displays. The OnePlus 12 is anticipated to feature a high refresh rate display, possibly up to 120Hz or higher, providing users with an incredibly fluid and seamless user experience. Whether you're scrolling through web pages, navigating the user interface, or playing games, the higher refresh rate of the OnePlus 12's display ensures that every interaction feels smooth and responsive.

Benefits of High Refresh Rate Displays:

- Smoother Animations: A higher refresh rate results in smoother animations and transitions, making the user interface feel more fluid and responsive.

- Reduced Motion Blur: Higher refresh rates help to reduce motion blur, resulting in clearer and more detailed visuals, particularly during fast-paced gaming or video playback.

- Improved Touch Response: High refresh rate displays offer improved touch response, reducing input latency and making interactions feel more immediate and precise.

- Enhanced Gaming Experience: Gamers can benefit from higher refresh rates, as it allows for smoother gameplay and reduced input lag, resulting in a more immersive and enjoyable gaming experience.

HDR Support: HDR (High Dynamic Range) support enhances the visual experience by expanding the range of colors and contrast levels that can be displayed on the screen. The OnePlus 12 is expected to feature HDR support, possibly HDR10+ or Dolby Vision, allowing users to enjoy HDR content from streaming services like Netflix, Amazon Prime Video, and YouTube. With HDR support, colors appear more vibrant, highlights are brighter, and shadows are deeper, resulting in a more lifelike and immersive viewing experience.

Benefits of HDR Support:

- Expanded Color Gamut: HDR support allows for a wider color gamut, resulting in more accurate and vibrant colors that closely resemble real-world visuals.

- Improved Contrast: HDR content features higher contrast ratios, with brighter highlights and darker shadows, resulting in greater detail and depth in the image.
- Enhanced Viewing Experience: HDR support enhances the overall viewing experience, making content appear more lifelike and immersive, whether you're watching movies, playing games, or viewing photos.

Optimized Display Settings: OnePlus devices typically offer a range of display settings that allow users to customize their viewing experience to suit their preferences. This includes options to adjust refresh rate settings, enable HDR enhancements, and fine-tune color calibration to achieve the desired visual effect. Whether you're a casual user or a content creator, the OnePlus 12's display settings can be tailored to meet your specific needs and preferences.

The OnePlus 12 is expected to feature a high refresh rate display and HDR support, providing users with a smoother and more immersive viewing experience. Whether you're watching movies, playing games, or browsing the web, the OnePlus 12's display technology ensures that content appears vibrant, detailed, and true to life, setting a new standard for smartphone displays.

Color Accuracy and Brightness

Color accuracy and brightness are critical factors that contribute to the overall visual quality and user experience of a smartphone display. OnePlus has consistently prioritized color accuracy and brightness in its smartphone displays, ensuring that users can enjoy vibrant and true-to-life visuals in various lighting conditions. With the OnePlus 12, users can expect further advancements in color accuracy and brightness to deliver an even more immersive viewing experience.

Color Accuracy: OnePlus devices are known for their color-accurate displays, which reproduce colors with precision and fidelity. The OnePlus 12 is anticipated to feature a display that is calibrated to industry-standard color profiles, ensuring that colors appear natural and true to life. Whether you're viewing photos, watching videos, or playing games, the OnePlus 12's display accurately represents the intended colors, allowing you to experience content as it was meant to be seen.

Benefits of Color Accuracy:

- True-to-Life Colors: Color-accurate displays reproduce colors with accuracy and fidelity, ensuring that content appears as the creator intended.

- Consistent Viewing Experience: With color-accurate displays, colors remain consistent across different devices and viewing conditions, allowing for a more cohesive and enjoyable viewing experience.

- Enhanced Productivity: Color-accurate displays are

essential for professionals who rely on accurate color reproduction for tasks such as photo editing, graphic design, and video production. The OnePlus 12's display ensures that colors are displayed accurately, allowing professionals to work with confidence and precision.

Brightness: The brightness of a smartphone display is crucial for visibility in various lighting conditions, including bright outdoor sunlight and dim indoor environments. The OnePlus 12 is expected to feature a high maximum brightness level, ensuring excellent visibility even in bright sunlight. Additionally, OnePlus devices typically include adaptive brightness technology, which automatically adjusts the screen brightness based on ambient lighting conditions to optimize visibility and battery life.

Benefits of Brightness:

- Enhanced Visibility: A bright display ensures excellent visibility, even in bright outdoor environments, allowing users to comfortably view content and interact with their device without straining their eyes.

- Improved Readability: With high brightness levels, text and graphics appear crisp and clear, enhancing readability and reducing eye strain, particularly during extended periods of use.

- Optimized Battery Life: OnePlus devices utilize adaptive brightness technology to adjust screen brightness dynamically based on ambient lighting conditions, optimizing visibility while minimizing battery consumption. This ensures that users can enjoy a bright and vibrant display without compromising on battery life.

Sunlight Readability: OnePlus devices typically feature enhanced sunlight readability technology, which improves screen visibility in bright outdoor environments. Whether you're reading emails, navigating maps, or watching videos, the OnePlus 12's display ensures that content remains visible and legible even under direct sunlight, providing a seamless and uninterrupted user experience.

Overall, the OnePlus 12 is expected to feature a display that excels in color accuracy and brightness, delivering vibrant and true-to-life visuals in various lighting conditions. Whether you're indoors or outdoors, the OnePlus 12's display ensures that content appears vivid, clear, and immersive, allowing you to enjoy an exceptional viewing experience wherever you go.

Chapter Four: Performance and Hardware

Processor and GPU

The processor and GPU (Graphics Processing Unit) are two of the most critical components that determine the performance capabilities of a smartphone, including speed, responsiveness, and graphical rendering. OnePlus has a history of equipping its devices with top-of-the-line processors and GPUs to deliver a smooth and powerful user experience. With the OnePlus 12, users can expect the latest advancements in processor and GPU technology to push the boundaries of performance even further.

Qualcomm Snapdragon Processor: OnePlus smartphones typically feature Qualcomm Snapdragon processors, renowned for their performance, efficiency, and reliability. The OnePlus 12 is anticipated to be powered by the latest Qualcomm Snapdragon chipset, delivering industry-leading performance and power efficiency. Whether you're multitasking, gaming, or streaming media, the OnePlus 12's Snapdragon processor ensures smooth and responsive performance for all your tasks.

Adreno GPU: Complementing the Snapdragon processor is the

Adreno GPU, which handles graphical rendering and ensures smooth and fluid visuals in games, videos, and other graphics-intensive applications. The OnePlus 12 is expected to feature a powerful Adreno GPU, capable of delivering stunning graphics and immersive gaming experiences. Whether you're playing the latest AAA titles or enjoying high-definition videos, the OnePlus 12's Adreno GPU ensures that visuals are rendered with precision and clarity.

Benefits of Snapdragon Processors:

- High Performance: Snapdragon processors offer industry-leading performance, allowing for seamless multitasking, faster app launches, and smoother overall user experience.

- Efficient Power Consumption: Snapdragon processors are known for their energy efficiency, striking a balance between performance and battery life to ensure long-lasting usage on a single charge.

- Optimized Connectivity: Snapdragon processors

feature integrated 5G modem technology, enabling lightning-fast download and upload speeds, low latency, and reliable connectivity for streaming, gaming, and other online activities.

Benefits of Adreno GPU:

- Smooth Graphics: The Adreno GPU delivers smooth and fluid graphics rendering, ensuring that games, videos, and animations appear crisp and responsive.

- Enhanced Gaming Performance: With the Adreno GPU, the OnePlus 12 offers enhanced gaming performance, allowing for high frame rates, detailed textures, and realistic lighting effects in games.

- Support for Advanced Graphics Technologies: The Adreno GPU supports advanced graphics technologies such as Vulkan API, OpenGL ES, and DirectX, enabling developers to create visually stunning and immersive gaming experiences on the OnePlus 12.

Optimized Software Integration: OnePlus optimizes its OxygenOS software to take full advantage of the capabilities of the Snapdragon processor and Adreno GPU. Through software optimizations, OnePlus ensures that the OnePlus 12 delivers a seamless and responsive user experience, with smooth performance and efficient power management across all tasks and applications.

Overall, the OnePlus 12's powerful Snapdragon processor and Adreno GPU combine to deliver exceptional performance and graphics capabilities, allowing users to enjoy smooth multitasking, immersive gaming, and seamless multimedia experiences. Whether you're a casual user or a power user, the OnePlus 12's performance hardware ensures that you can tackle any task with ease and efficiency.

RAM and Storage Options:

The RAM (Random Access Memory) and storage options available in a smartphone significantly impact its performance, multitasking capabilities, and storage capacity for apps, media, and files. OnePlus is known for offering generous RAM and storage configurations in its devices, catering to the diverse needs and preferences of users. With the OnePlus 12, users can expect a range of RAM and storage options to suit their requirements, whether they prioritize multitasking, gaming, or media consumption.

RAM Options: OnePlus devices typically offer multiple RAM configurations to accommodate different usage scenarios and performance requirements. The OnePlus 12 is expected to be available in a range of RAM options, including:

- 8GB RAM: Suitable for everyday use, including web browsing, social media, and light multitasking. Users can expect smooth performance and responsive app launches with 8GB of RAM.

- 12GB RAM: Ideal for power users, gamers, and multitaskers who demand exceptional performance and responsiveness. With 12GB of RAM, the OnePlus 12 can handle intensive multitasking, gaming, and productivity tasks with ease.

- 16GB RAM (Possibly): For users who require the ultimate in performance and multitasking capabilities, OnePlus may offer a higher-tier variant of the OnePlus 12 with 16GB of RAM. This configuration provides ample headroom for running multiple apps simultaneously, editing large files, and gaming at the highest settings.

Storage Options: In addition to varying RAM configurations, OnePlus devices typically offer multiple storage options to accommodate users' storage needs for apps, photos, videos, and other media. The OnePlus 12 is expected to be available in a range of storage capacities, including:

- 128GB Storage: Suitable for most users who require ample storage for apps, photos, videos, and other media. With 128GB of storage, users have plenty of space to store their favorite apps, games, and multimedia content without worrying about running out of space.

- 256GB Storage: Ideal for users who require even more storage capacity for storing large files, downloading offline media, and installing a vast library of apps and games. With 256GB of storage, users have ample room to store their entire digital library and more.

- 512GB Storage (Possibly): For users with extensive storage needs, OnePlus may offer a higher-tier variant of the OnePlus 12 with 512GB of storage. This configuration provides abundant storage space for storing large files, downloading offline media, and installing a vast array of apps and games without compromise.

Expandable Storage (Possibly): While OnePlus devices traditionally do not feature expandable storage via microSD cards, OnePlus may introduce this feature with the OnePlus 12 to offer users additional flexibility in expanding their device's storage capacity. Expandable storage allows users to insert a microSD card to supplement the device's internal storage, providing even more space for apps, photos, videos, and other media.

Optimized Storage Management: OnePlus devices typically feature optimized storage management capabilities to help users maximize available storage space and enhance device performance. This includes features such as intelligent app management, cache cleaning, and storage optimization tools that help users identify and remove unnecessary files and apps to free up space and improve performance.

Overall, the OnePlus 12 is expected to offer a range of RAM and storage options to suit the diverse needs and preferences of users. Whether you prioritize multitasking, gaming, or media consumption, the OnePlus 12's generous RAM and storage configurations ensure that you have the performance and storage capacity you need to stay productive and entertained on the go.

Benchmark Performance

Benchmark performance is a crucial aspect that provides objective insights into a smartphone's computational power, graphics rendering capabilities, and overall system performance. OnePlus devices have consistently performed well in benchmark tests, thanks to their powerful hardware components and optimized software integration. With the OnePlus 12, users can expect impressive benchmark performance that demonstrates the device's capability to handle demanding tasks with ease.

Anticipated Benchmark Tests: The OnePlus 12 is expected to undergo a series of benchmark tests to evaluate its performance across various metrics. Some of the most commonly used benchmark tests include:

- Geekbench: Geekbench evaluates CPU performance by measuring single-core and multi-core processing speeds. Higher scores indicate better CPU performance, reflecting improved responsiveness and multitasking capabilities.

- 3DMark: 3DMark assesses GPU performance by measuring graphics rendering capabilities in gaming scenarios. Higher scores indicate better graphics performance, ensuring smooth and immersive gaming experiences with high frame rates and detailed visuals.

- AnTuTu Benchmark: AnTuTu Benchmark provides an overall performance score based on CPU, GPU, memory, and storage performance. Higher scores indicate better overall system performance, indicating the device's ability to handle multitasking, gaming, and other intensive tasks effectively.

- PCMark: PCMark evaluates overall system performance by simulating real-world usage scenarios such as web browsing, video editing, and photo editing. Higher scores indicate smoother and more responsive performance across various productivity tasks and multimedia activities.

Expected Performance Improvements: The OnePlus 12 is anticipated to deliver significant performance improvements compared to its predecessors, thanks to advancements in hardware and software optimization. Some of the key areas where users can expect performance enhancements include:

- CPU Performance: With the latest Qualcomm Snapdragon chipset and generous RAM configurations, the OnePlus 12 is expected to offer improved CPU performance, resulting in faster app launches, smoother multitasking, and improved overall responsiveness.

- GPU Performance: The OnePlus 12's Adreno GPU is anticipated to deliver enhanced graphics rendering capabilities, allowing for more immersive gaming experiences with higher frame rates, detailed textures, and realistic lighting effects.

- Memory Management: OnePlus devices typically excel in memory management, with efficient RAM utilization and optimized app management. The OnePlus 12 is expected to continue this trend, ensuring smooth and responsive performance even during intensive multitasking scenarios.

- Software Optimization: OxygenOS, OnePlus's custom Android-based operating system, is known for its lightweight and optimized performance. The OnePlus 12 is expected to run the latest version of OxygenOS, featuring further refinements and optimizations to enhance overall system performance and responsiveness.

Real-World Performance: While benchmark tests provide valuable insights into a device's performance capabilities, real-world usage scenarios ultimately determine the user experience. The OnePlus 12's impressive benchmark performance is expected to translate into a seamless and responsive user experience across various tasks, including gaming, multimedia consumption, productivity, and multitasking.

Future-Proof Performance: OnePlus devices are designed to deliver long-lasting performance and reliability, ensuring that users can enjoy a smooth and responsive user experience for years to come. The OnePlus 12's powerful hardware components and optimized software integration position it as a future-proof device capable of meeting the performance demands of tomorrow's apps, games, and multimedia content.

Overall, the OnePlus 12's anticipated benchmark performance reflects its commitment to delivering powerful hardware, optimized software, and a seamless user experience. Whether you're gaming, multitasking, or enjoying multimedia content, the OnePlus 12's impressive performance capabilities ensure that you can tackle any task with confidence and efficiency.

Cooling System

A robust cooling system is essential for maintaining optimal performance and preventing thermal throttling in smartphones, especially during prolonged and intensive usage scenarios such as gaming or multitasking. OnePlus devices typically incorporate advanced cooling solutions to dissipate heat effectively and ensure consistent performance under heavy workloads. With the OnePlus 12, users can expect a sophisticated cooling system designed to keep the device cool and responsive even during demanding tasks.

Vapor Chamber Cooling: OnePlus devices often utilize vapor chamber cooling technology, which consists of a thin chamber filled with a special coolant that absorbs and dissipates heat away from the device's internal components. The OnePlus 12 is expected to feature an upgraded vapor chamber cooling system, with enhanced thermal conductivity and efficiency to effectively manage heat generation during intensive tasks.

Graphite Heat Dissipation: In addition to vapor chamber cooling, OnePlus devices may incorporate graphite heat dissipation materials into their design. Graphite sheets or layers are strategically placed within the device to absorb and distribute heat away from critical components, ensuring more uniform temperature distribution and preventing hotspots that could impact performance.

Copper Heat Pipes: Some high-end smartphones, including previous OnePlus models, feature copper heat pipes as part of their cooling solutions. Copper is an excellent conductor of heat, and heat pipes help transfer heat away from the CPU, GPU, and other heat-generating components to the device's exterior, where it can be dissipated more efficiently.

Optimized Thermal Design: OnePlus engineers meticulously design the internal layout and thermal architecture of their devices to maximize airflow and heat dissipation. This includes strategically placing components, optimizing the positioning of heat-generating elements, and designing ventilation pathways to facilitate efficient heat transfer and dissipation.

Dynamic Thermal Management: OnePlus devices may feature dynamic thermal management systems that adjust CPU and GPU performance based on temperature sensors and workload demands. By dynamically scaling performance levels in response to changing thermal conditions, OnePlus ensures consistent performance and prevents overheating or thermal throttling during intensive tasks.

Software Optimization: OxygenOS, OnePlus's custom Android-based operating system, may include software optimizations to complement the device's cooling hardware. This may include intelligent thermal management algorithms, power-saving features, and performance optimizations that work in tandem with the cooling system to ensure smooth and responsive performance under all usage scenarios.

User Experience: A well-designed cooling system not only ensures optimal performance but also enhances the user experience by keeping the device cool and comfortable to hold during extended usage sessions. Whether you're gaming, streaming, or multitasking, the OnePlus 12's advanced cooling system ensures that the device remains responsive and reliable, even under demanding conditions.

Overall, the OnePlus 12 is expected to feature a sophisticated cooling system comprising vapor chamber cooling, graphite heat dissipation, copper heat pipes, optimized thermal design, dynamic thermal management, and software optimization. By effectively managing heat generation and dissipation, the OnePlus 12 delivers consistent performance and ensures a smooth and enjoyable user experience, even during the most demanding tasks.

Chapter Five: Software and User Interface

OxygenOS Features

OxygenOS is OnePlus's custom Android-based operating system known for its clean, intuitive interface, smooth performance, and extensive customization options. With each iteration, OnePlus introduces new features and enhancements to OxygenOS, enriching the user experience and adding value to its devices. The OnePlus 12 is expected to come pre-installed with the latest version of OxygenOS, offering a plethora of innovative features designed to enhance productivity, customization, and overall user satisfaction.

Smooth Performance: OxygenOS is renowned for its smooth and responsive performance, thanks to optimizations that prioritize speed and efficiency. With the OnePlus 12, users can expect buttery-smooth animations, fast app launches, and seamless multitasking, ensuring a fluid and enjoyable user experience.

Clean User Interface: OxygenOS features a clean and minimalist user interface that prioritizes simplicity and ease of use. The interface is designed to be intuitive and clutter-free, allowing users to navigate their device with ease and access essential features and settings without unnecessary distractions.

Customization Options: One of the standout features of OxygenOS is its extensive customization options, allowing users to personalize their device to suit their preferences. From customizable themes and icon packs to advanced customization settings for the status bar, navigation gestures, and quick settings panel, OxygenOS empowers users to tailor their device's look and feel to match their unique style.

Gestures and Navigation: OxygenOS offers a range of intuitive gestures and navigation shortcuts to streamline user interactions and enhance usability. Users can perform actions such as launching the camera, taking screenshots, or accessing the notification shade with simple gestures, eliminating the need for physical buttons and making one-handed use more convenient.

Zen Mode: Zen Mode is a unique feature of OxygenOS designed to promote digital wellness and mindfulness by temporarily disabling non-essential features and notifications. Users can activate Zen Mode to take a break from their device and focus on other activities without distractions, helping to reduce screen time and promote a healthier balance between digital and offline activities.

Gaming Mode: Gaming Mode optimizes the gaming experience on the OnePlus 12 by prioritizing performance, minimizing distractions, and enhancing audiovisual quality. Users can customize Gaming Mode settings to block notifications, optimize network connectivity, and fine-tune performance settings for a smoother and more immersive gaming experience.

Smart Features: OxygenOS incorporates a range of smart features and optimizations to enhance productivity and convenience. This includes features such as Reading Mode for reducing eye strain, Parallel Apps for running multiple instances of the same app, and OnePlus Shelf for quick access to frequently used apps, contacts, and widgets.

Software Updates: OnePlus is committed to providing timely software updates and security patches to ensure that users continue to receive the latest features, enhancements, and security fixes for their devices. With OxygenOS, users can expect regular updates that further improve performance, stability, and user experience over time.

Overall, OxygenOS on the OnePlus 12 offers a compelling blend of smooth performance, clean design, extensive customization options, and innovative features designed to enhance productivity, convenience, and digital well-being. Whether you're a power user, a casual gamer, or someone who values simplicity and ease of use, OxygenOS delivers a user experience that is both intuitive and enjoyable, setting OnePlus devices apart in the crowded smartphone market.

Customization Options

One of the hallmarks of OxygenOS, the custom Android-based operating system developed by OnePlus, is its extensive range of customization options. These features empower users to personalize their device's look, feel, and functionality according to their preferences, creating a more tailored and enjoyable user experience. With the OnePlus 12, users can expect a wide array of customization options that allow them to make their device truly their own.

Themes and Icon Packs: OxygenOS offers a variety of

themes and icon packs that users can choose from to customize the appearance of their device's home screen and app icons. Whether you prefer a minimalist design, vibrant colors, or something more whimsical, OxygenOS provides ample options to suit every taste.

Customizable Home Screen Layout: Users can customize their device's home screen layout by arranging app icons, widgets, and shortcuts to their liking. OxygenOS allows for flexible grid sizes, allowing users to adjust the number of apps and widgets displayed on each home screen page for a personalized layout.

Customizable Status Bar: OxygenOS provides extensive customization options for the status bar, allowing users to choose which icons and indicators are displayed, adjust the clock style and position, and enable/disable status bar icons for notifications, battery, and connectivity.

Navigation Gestures: OnePlus devices offer navigation gesture controls that allow users to navigate their device using intuitive swipe gestures instead of traditional on-screen navigation buttons. Users can customize gesture settings to perform actions such as back, home, and recent apps with simple swipes, enhancing one-handed usability and reducing screen clutter.

Quick Settings Customization: OxygenOS allows users to customize the quick settings panel by rearranging toggles, adding/removing quick settings tiles, and adjusting the layout to prioritize frequently used functions. This enables users to access essential settings and controls with greater efficiency and convenience.

Customizable Buttons and Shortcuts: OnePlus devices offer options to customize hardware buttons and create custom shortcuts for launching apps or performing specific actions. Users can remap the functionality of the power button, volume keys, and alert slider to suit their preferences, providing greater flexibility and control over their device's interactions.

Font and Display Customization: OxygenOS includes options to customize font styles, sizes, and display scaling to optimize readability and visual comfort. Users can choose from a selection of pre-installed fonts or download additional fonts from the OnePlus

Font Store to personalize their device's typography.

App Drawer Customization: OxygenOS allows users to customize the app drawer layout, including options to organize apps alphabetically, by category, or manually arrange them according to preference. Users can also enable/disable the app drawer search bar and adjust other app drawer settings to streamline app management and navigation.

Dark Mode and Accent Colors: OxygenOS offers a system-wide dark mode that transforms the user interface into a dark color scheme for reduced eye strain and improved battery life, particularly on devices with AMOLED displays. Users can also customize accent colors to personalize the appearance of system UI elements such as buttons, sliders, and highlights.

Scheduled Themes: OxygenOS includes the option to schedule theme changes based on time of day or sunrise/sunset, allowing users to automatically switch between light and dark themes or different color schemes based on their preferences or ambient lighting conditions.

OxygenOS provides a wealth of customization options that empower users to tailor their device's appearance, functionality, and user experience to match their individual preferences and lifestyle. Whether you're a minimalist who prefers a clean and simple interface or a power user who enjoys tinkering with every aspect of your device, OxygenOS offers the flexibility and versatility to create a truly personalized smartphone experience on the OnePlus 12.

Software updates play a vital role in ensuring the longevity, security, and performance of smartphones. OnePlus is known for its commitment to providing timely software updates and ongoing support for its devices, ensuring that users receive the latest features, enhancements, and security patches throughout the lifecycle of their device. With the OnePlus 12, users can expect a robust software update policy and comprehensive support ecosystem designed to enhance the overall user experience and satisfaction.

Timely Software Updates: OnePlus prioritizes timely software updates to ensure that users have access to the latest features, improvements, and security patches. The OnePlus 12 is expected to receive regular updates, including major Android OS upgrades, monthly security patches, and firmware updates to optimize performance, stability, and user experience.

Android OS Upgrades: OnePlus devices typically receive at least two major Android OS upgrades during their lifecycle, ensuring that users can enjoy the latest Android features and improvements. With the OnePlus 12, users can expect to receive timely upgrades to new Android versions, providing access to new functionalities, design changes, and performance optimizations.

Security Patches: OnePlus prioritizes the security of its devices and regularly releases monthly security patches to address potential vulnerabilities and security threats. These updates are designed to protect user data and ensure the integrity of the device's software ecosystem. The OnePlus 12 is expected to receive prompt security updates to keep users protected against emerging security risks.

Firmware Updates: In addition to Android OS upgrades and security patches, OnePlus devices receive periodic firmware updates to optimize performance, enhance device functionality, and address hardware-specific issues. These updates may include improvements to camera performance, battery life, connectivity, and other system-level optimizations.

Open Beta Program: OnePlus offers an Open Beta Program for users who want to test upcoming software releases and provide feedback to OnePlus developers. Participants in the Open Beta Program have the opportunity to try out new features and improvements before they are officially rolled out to the wider user base, contributing to the refinement and optimization of OnePlus software.

Community Feedback: OnePlus values community feedback and actively engages with users through its online forums, social media channels, and customer support channels. Users can provide feedback, report bugs, and suggest new features, helping to shape the direction of future software updates and improvements.

Extended Support: OnePlus typically provides extended support for its devices beyond the initial warranty period, ensuring that users continue to receive software updates and security patches for an extended period.

This commitment to long-term support enhances the value proposition of OnePlus devices and fosters loyalty among users.

User-Friendly Update Process: OnePlus strives to make the software update process as seamless and user-friendly as possible. Updates can be downloaded and installed over-the-air (OTA) directly on the device, with clear instructions and notifications provided to guide users through the update process.

Overall, OnePlus is dedicated to providing timely software updates and ongoing support for its devices, ensuring that users can enjoy a secure, stable, and optimized user experience with the OnePlus 12. Whether it's major Android OS upgrades, monthly security patches, or firmware optimizations, OnePlus remains committed to enhancing the overall user experience and satisfaction throughout the lifecycle of its devices.

Chapter Six: Camera System

Rear Camera Setup

The rear camera setup of a smartphone plays a pivotal role in capturing high-quality photos and videos, allowing users to preserve memories, express creativity, and share moments with friends and family. OnePlus has continually innovated its camera technology, incorporating advanced imaging capabilities and cutting-edge features to deliver exceptional photography experiences. With the OnePlus 12, users can expect an upgraded rear camera setup that raises the bar in terms of image quality, versatility, and performance.

Primary Camera: The primary camera is the cornerstone of the rear camera setup, responsible for capturing detailed and vibrant photos in various lighting conditions. The OnePlus 12 is expected to feature a high-resolution primary sensor with advanced pixel technology and optical enhancements to deliver sharp, lifelike images with accurate colors and fine details.

Ultra-Wide Camera: In addition to the primary camera, the OnePlus 12 is likely to include an ultra-wide-angle camera that expands the creative possibilities by offering a wider field of view.

The ultra-wide camera enables users to capture expansive landscapes, group photos, and architectural shots with a unique perspective, adding depth and drama to their photography.

Telephoto or Depth Sensor (Possibly): Depending on the configuration, the OnePlus 12 may include a telephoto lens for optical zoom capabilities or a depth sensor for capturing portrait photos with natural background blur (bokeh) effects. These additional sensors enhance the versatility of the camera system, allowing users to capture stunning portraits, close-up shots, and distant subjects with clarity and detail.

Advanced Imaging Features: OnePlus devices are known for their advanced imaging features and software enhancements that elevate the photography experience. The OnePlus 12 is expected to introduce new and improved camera features, including:

- Night Mode: Enhanced low-light photography capabilities for capturing bright and clear photos in dimly lit environments without the need for a flash.

- Pro Mode: Manual camera controls that allow users to adjust settings such as ISO, shutter speed, and white balance for fine-tuning exposure and achieving creative effects.

- AI Scene Recognition: Intelligent scene detection and optimization that automatically adjusts camera settings based on the subject and shooting conditions to ensure optimal image quality.

- HDR (High Dynamic Range): Enhanced HDR capabilities for capturing photos with balanced exposure and dynamic range, preserving detail in both highlights and shadows.

- Super Macro Mode: Close-up photography mode that allows users to capture intricate details and textures with exceptional clarity and magnification.

- Slow Motion and Time-Lapse: High-quality slow-motion and time-lapse video recording modes for creating captivating videos with unique visual effects and storytelling potential.

Optical Image Stabilization (OIS) and Electronic Image Stabilization (EIS): The OnePlus 12 is likely to feature advanced stabilization technologies such as OIS and EIS to minimize camera shake and motion blur, resulting in sharper photos and smoother video footage, even in challenging shooting conditions or while on the move.

AI-Powered Enhancements: OnePlus devices leverage artificial intelligence (AI) to enhance camera performance and image quality. AI-powered features such as scene recognition, smart exposure adjustment, and real-time image processing help users capture stunning photos with minimal effort, ensuring that every shot looks its best.

Video Recording Capabilities: The OnePlus 12 is expected to offer high-quality video recording capabilities, including 4K resolution at various frame rates, slow-motion video recording, and advanced video stabilization. Users can capture cinematic-quality videos with rich detail, vibrant colors, and smooth motion, making the OnePlus 12 a versatile tool for both photography and videography.

Overall, the rear camera setup of the OnePlus 12 is anticipated to deliver exceptional imaging capabilities, versatility, and performance, empowering users to unleash their creativity and capture memorable moments with stunning clarity and detail. Whether you're a photography enthusiast, social media influencer, or casual shooter, the OnePlus 12's advanced camera system ensures that you can capture every moment with confidence and precision.

Ultra-Wide and Telephoto Lenses

The inclusion of ultra-wide and telephoto lenses in a smartphone's camera system expands its capabilities, offering users greater flexibility and creative freedom in photography. These additional lenses complement the primary camera, enabling users to capture a wider field of view with the ultra-wide lens and zoom in on distant subjects with the telephoto lens. With the OnePlus 12, users can expect an enhanced camera setup that includes both ultra-wide and telephoto lenses, unlocking new possibilities for capturing stunning photos and videos.

Ultra-Wide Lens:

- The ultra-wide lens on the OnePlus 12 provides a significantly wider field of view compared to the primary camera, allowing users to capture expansive landscapes, group shots, and architectural scenes with ease.

- With its wide-angle perspective, the ultra-wide lens adds depth and drama to photos, creating dynamic compositions and emphasizing spatial relationships between subjects.

- The OnePlus 12's ultra-wide lens is expected to feature advanced optical design and image correction algorithms to minimize distortion and ensure edge-to-edge sharpness, resulting in high-quality images with accurate proportions and minimal aberrations.

- Ultra-wide lenses are particularly useful for capturing immersive photos and videos that convey a sense of scale and perspective, making them ideal for travel photography, outdoor adventures, and architectural photography.

Telephoto Lens:

- The telephoto lens on the OnePlus 12 offers optical zoom capabilities, allowing users to magnify distant subjects and capture detailed shots without sacrificing image quality.

- With its zoom functionality, the telephoto lens enables users to get closer to the action, whether it's capturing wildlife, sports events, or candid portraits from a distance.

- The OnePlus 12's telephoto lens is expected to feature optical image stabilization (OIS) to minimize camera shake and ensure sharp, blur-free images even when shooting handheld at high magnification levels.

- Telephoto lenses are invaluable for achieving creative effects such as shallow depth of field and background compression, enabling users to isolate subjects against a blurred background and create visually striking portraits with smooth bokeh effects.

Dual-Lens Photography:

- By combining the capabilities of the ultra-wide and telephoto lenses with the primary camera, the OnePlus 12 offers users a versatile triple-lens camera system that covers a wide range of focal lengths and shooting scenarios.

- Users can seamlessly switch between lenses to capture different perspectives and compositions, from sweeping panoramas with the ultra-wide lens to detailed close-ups with the telephoto lens.
- The OnePlus 12's camera app is expected to feature intuitive controls and modes that leverage the unique capabilities of each lens, such as panorama mode for ultra-wide shots and portrait

mode for telephoto portraits with creamy bokeh.

Enhanced Photography Experience:

- With the ultra-wide and telephoto lenses, the OnePlus 12 delivers an enhanced photography experience that empowers users to unleash their creativity and capture moments from new perspectives.

- Whether it's capturing breathtaking landscapes, zooming in on distant subjects, or experimenting with creative compositions, the OnePlus 12's versatile camera system ensures that users can capture every moment with precision and artistic flair.

Overall, the inclusion of ultra-wide and telephoto lenses in the OnePlus 12's camera system expands its photographic capabilities, offering users greater versatility and creative potential in capturing stunning photos and videos. Whether you're an avid traveler, aspiring photographer, or content creator, the OnePlus 12's triple-lens camera system provides the tools you need to express your vision and tell your story with clarity and impact.

Camera Software Features

The software features of a smartphone's camera play a crucial role in enhancing the user experience, optimizing image quality, and providing creative tools for photography and videography. OnePlus has a history of incorporating innovative camera software features into its devices, leveraging advanced algorithms and artificial intelligence to deliver exceptional results. With the OnePlus 12, users can expect a comprehensive suite of camera software features designed to elevate their photography and videography experience to new heights.

Night Mode:

- Night Mode is a flagship feature of OnePlus devices that enhances low-light photography by capturing multiple exposures and merging them into a single, well-exposed image with reduced noise and improved detail.

- The OnePlus 12's Night Mode is expected to leverage advanced image processing algorithms and machine learning techniques to optimize exposure, color balance, and detail preservation in low-light conditions, allowing users to

capture bright and clear
photos even in challenging
lighting situations.

Pro Mode:

- Pro Mode offers manual
  camera controls that allow
  users to adjust settings such
  as ISO, shutter speed, white
  balance, and focus manually,
  providing greater flexibility
  and control over the
  exposure and composition
  of their photos.
- With Pro Mode on the
  OnePlus 12, users can
  fine-tune camera settings to
  achieve their desired artistic
  effects, whether it's

capturing long-exposure light trails, freezing fast-moving subjects, or achieving precise color reproduction in challenging lighting conditions.

HDR (High Dynamic Range):

- HDR mode enhances the dynamic range of photos by combining multiple exposures to preserve detail in both highlights and shadows, resulting in balanced and natural-looking images with improved contrast and tonal range.

- The OnePlus 12's HDR mode is expected to offer real-time

HDR processing, allowing users to capture well-exposed photos with vibrant colors and lifelike contrast, even in scenes with high contrast and uneven lighting.

AI Scene Recognition:

- AI Scene Recognition automatically detects the subject and scene type in real-time and applies optimized camera settings and image processing algorithms to enhance image quality and color reproduction.

- The OnePlus 12's AI Scene Recognition is likely to recognize a wide range of scenes and subjects, including landscapes, portraits, food, pets, and more, ensuring that users can capture stunning photos with minimal effort and maximum impact.

Super Macro Mode:

- Super Macro Mode enables users to capture extreme close-up shots with exceptional detail and clarity, allowing them to explore the microscopic world and capture intricate textures and patterns with stunning realism.

- The OnePlus 12's Super Macro Mode may leverage advanced focusing algorithms and image processing techniques to achieve sharp focus and accurate color reproduction at close distances, resulting in breathtaking macro photos that reveal the beauty of the smallest details.

Portrait Mode:

- Portrait Mode creates professional-looking portraits with natural background blur (bokeh) effects, simulating the shallow depth of field typically associated with high-end DSLR cameras and professional lenses.

- The OnePlus 12's Portrait Mode is expected to offer advanced depth sensing and segmentation algorithms to accurately separate the subject from the background and apply realistic bokeh effects, resulting in studio-quality portraits that stand out from the crowd.

Slow Motion and Time-Lapse:

- Slow Motion and Time-Lapse modes allow

users to capture creative videos with unique visual effects and storytelling potential.

- The OnePlus 12's Slow Motion and Time-Lapse modes are likely to offer adjustable frame rates, resolution settings, and playback speeds, giving users full control over the timing and pacing of their videos for cinematic-quality results.

Smart Filters and Effects:

- Smart Filters and Effects provide users with a variety of creative options for enhancing their photos and videos, including artistic filters, color effects, and beauty enhancements.

- The OnePlus 12's camera app may include a selection of built-in filters and effects that users can apply in real-time or during post-processing, allowing them to add personality and style to their photos and videos with a single tap.

AI-Powered Enhancements:

- OnePlus devices leverage artificial intelligence (AI) to enhance image quality and optimize camera performance in various shooting scenarios.

- The OnePlus 12's camera software may include AI-powered features such as intelligent noise reduction, scene optimization, and face detection autofocus, ensuring that users can capture stunning photos with minimal effort and maximum impact.

Multi-Lens Integration:

- The OnePlus 12's camera app is expected to seamlessly integrate the capabilities of the primary, ultra-wide, and telephoto lenses, allowing users to switch between lenses and capture different perspectives with ease.

- Multi-lens integration enables features such as seamless zooming between lenses, panoramic photo stitching, and multi-frame composition, ensuring that users can leverage the full potential of the OnePlus 12's triple-lens camera system for creative photography and videography.

Overall, the OnePlus 12's camera software features are designed to enhance the user experience, optimize image quality, and provide creative tools for capturing stunning photos and videos in any situation. Whether you're a photography enthusiast, social media influencer, or casual shooter, the OnePlus 12's advanced camera software ensures that you can unleash your creativity and capture every moment with precision and style.

Sample Image and Video Quality

The image and video quality of a smartphone's camera are paramount, as they directly impact the user's ability to capture and preserve memories with clarity and detail. OnePlus has continuously improved the camera technology in its devices, striving to deliver exceptional image and video quality that rivals dedicated digital cameras. With the OnePlus 12, users can expect superior image and video quality across a variety of shooting scenarios, thanks to advanced camera hardware and software optimizations.

Daylight Photography:

- In daylight conditions, the OnePlus 12's camera excels at capturing vibrant and detailed images with accurate colors and natural-looking tones. The primary camera's high-resolution sensor, combined with advanced image processing algorithms, ensures that every shot is sharp and well-balanced, with excellent dynamic range and contrast.

- The ultra-wide lens expands the creative possibilities by capturing expansive landscapes and group shots with a wider field of view, while maintaining edge-to-edge sharpness and minimal distortion.

- Sample images taken with the OnePlus 12 in daylight conditions showcase the device's ability to capture rich textures, fine details, and vivid colors, whether it's a scenic landscape, a bustling city street, or a close-up shot of a flower in bloom.

Low-Light Photography:

- In low-light conditions, the OnePlus 12's camera shines with its advanced night mode capabilities, allowing users to capture bright and clear photos with reduced noise and improved detail, even in challenging lighting situations.

- Night mode leverages multi-frame image processing and computational photography techniques to merge multiple exposures and enhance overall image quality, resulting in stunning photos that rival those taken with a dedicated camera.

- Sample images taken with the OnePlus 12 in low-light conditions demonstrate the device's ability to capture well-exposed photos with minimal noise and maximum detail, whether it's a city skyline at dusk, a dimly lit indoor scene, or a nighttime portrait under streetlights.

Portrait Photography:

- Portrait mode on the OnePlus 12 creates professional-looking portraits with natural background blur (bokeh) effects, highlighting the subject and adding depth and dimension to the image.

- The OnePlus 12's portrait mode utilizes advanced depth sensing and segmentation algorithms to accurately separate the subject from the background, ensuring precise edge detection and realistic bokeh rendering.

- Sample portrait images taken with the OnePlus 12 showcase the device's ability to capture studio-quality portraits with creamy bokeh effects, sharp subject detail, and lifelike skin tones, whether it's a close-up headshot, a candid street portrait, or a group photo with friends.

Video Recording:

- The OnePlus 12 offers high-quality video recording capabilities, allowing users to capture cinematic-quality videos with smooth motion, vibrant colors, and crisp detail.

- The device supports 4K video recording at various frame rates, enabling users to capture ultra-high-definition footage with stunning clarity and realism.

- Video stabilization technology, including optical image stabilization (OIS) and electronic image stabilization (EIS), ensures that videos are steady and shake-free, even when shooting handheld or in motion.

- Sample videos recorded with the OnePlus 12 demonstrate the device's ability to capture dynamic and immersive footage, whether it's a scenic travel montage, a fast-paced action sequence, or a heartfelt family moment.

Overall, the OnePlus 12 delivers exceptional image and video quality that exceeds expectations, allowing users to capture and preserve moments with clarity, detail, and realism. Whether you're an amateur photographer, a social media influencer, or a professional videographer, the OnePlus 12's advanced camera technology ensures that you can unleash your creativity and

capture every moment with precision
and style.

Chapter Seven: Battery Life and Charging

Battery Capacity

The battery capacity of a smartphone is a critical factor in determining its overall battery life and endurance. A higher capacity battery typically allows for longer usage between charges, providing users with the convenience of extended device usage without the need for frequent recharging. With the OnePlus 12, users can expect a substantial battery capacity that supports all-day usage and beyond, ensuring reliable performance throughout the day.

Enhanced Battery Capacity: The OnePlus 12 is anticipated to feature an enhanced battery capacity compared to its predecessors, allowing users to enjoy extended usage time without compromising on performance or functionality. With advancements in battery technology and device optimization, OnePlus aims to provide users with a battery that meets the demands of modern smartphone usage.

Optimized Power Efficiency: In addition to increasing battery capacity, OnePlus focuses on optimizing power efficiency throughout the device's hardware and software ecosystem. This includes efficient chipset design, intelligent power management algorithms, and software optimizations to minimize background battery drain and maximize standby time.

Usage Scenarios: The increased battery capacity of the OnePlus 12 ensures that users can comfortably use their device for a wide range of activities throughout the day without constantly worrying about running out of battery. Whether it's streaming videos, browsing the web, playing games, or multitasking between apps, the OnePlus 12's battery is designed to keep up with the demands of modern smartphone usage.

Typical Day-to-Day Usage: For typical day-to-day usage scenarios, including web browsing, social media usage, messaging, and occasional gaming or multimedia consumption, users can expect the OnePlus 12 to deliver all-day battery life on a single charge. The enhanced battery capacity ensures that users can confidently use their device throughout the day without needing to recharge until the end of the day.

Heavy Usage and Power Users: Even for power users who frequently engage in intensive tasks such as gaming, video streaming, or productivity workloads, the OnePlus 12's battery capacity provides sufficient endurance to keep up with demanding usage patterns. With fast charging capabilities, users can quickly recharge their device when needed, ensuring minimal downtime and maximum productivity.

Battery Longevity and Health: OnePlus prioritizes battery longevity and health by implementing features such as optimized charging algorithms, temperature monitoring, and battery health diagnostics. These features help prolong the lifespan of the battery and maintain its performance over time, ensuring that users can enjoy reliable battery performance throughout the lifecycle of the device.

Fast Charging Technology: In addition to battery capacity, the OnePlus 12 is expected to support fast charging technology, allowing users to recharge their device quickly and conveniently when needed. OnePlus's proprietary fast charging technology, such as Warp Charge, delivers fast and efficient charging speeds without compromising on battery health or safety.

Overall, the OnePlus 12's enhanced battery capacity, optimized power efficiency, and fast charging capabilities ensure that users can enjoy reliable battery life and convenient charging experiences, empowering them to stay connected and productive throughout the day without compromise.

Charging Speeds and Technology

Charging speed and technology are crucial aspects of a smartphone's battery experience, as they determine how quickly users can recharge their devices and get back to using them.

OnePlus has been at the forefront of fast charging technology, introducing innovative solutions to deliver rapid and efficient charging experiences. With the OnePlus 12, users can expect cutting-edge charging speeds and technology that minimize downtime and maximize convenience.

Warp Charge Technology:

- Warp Charge is OnePlus's proprietary fast charging technology, known for its industry-leading charging speeds and efficiency. With Warp Charge, users can quickly recharge their devices and get back to using them in no time.

- The OnePlus 12 is expected to feature the latest iteration of Warp Charge technology, offering even faster charging speeds and improved efficiency compared to previous generations. Whether it's topping up your battery before heading out or charging your device during a break, Warp Charge ensures that you can get the most out of your device with minimal waiting time.

Charging Speeds:

- The OnePlus 12 is anticipated to support blazing-fast charging speeds, allowing users to recharge their devices from zero to a significant percentage in a matter of minutes. With Warp Charge technology, users can expect rapid charging speeds that outpace conventional charging methods, ensuring that their device is always ready when they need it.

- The exact charging speeds of the OnePlus 12 may vary depending on factors such as battery capacity, charging cable, and power adapter specifications. However, OnePlus is committed to pushing the boundaries of charging technology to deliver the fastest and most efficient charging experiences possible.

Wired and Wireless Charging:

- While OnePlus devices have traditionally focused on wired charging solutions, the OnePlus 12 may also introduce advancements in wireless charging technology. Wireless charging offers the convenience of cable-free charging, allowing users to recharge their devices with ease using compatible wireless charging pads.

- The OnePlus 12's wireless charging capabilities, if included, are expected to deliver fast and efficient charging speeds that rival wired charging solutions, ensuring that users can enjoy the flexibility of wireless charging without sacrificing speed or performance.

Safety and Reliability:

- Safety and reliability are paramount when it comes to charging technology, and OnePlus prioritizes the implementation of advanced safety features to protect both the device and the user during the charging process.

- Warp Charge technology incorporates multiple layers of protection, including temperature monitoring, voltage regulation, and surge protection, to ensure safe and reliable charging experiences. Users can charge their devices with confidence, knowing that OnePlus's fast charging technology is designed with their safety in mind.

Smart Charging Management:

- OnePlus devices feature intelligent charging management systems that optimize the charging process based on factors such as battery health, usage patterns, and environmental conditions. These systems help prolong the lifespan of the battery and maintain its performance over time, ensuring that users can enjoy reliable battery performance throughout the lifecycle of the device.

- The OnePlus 12 is expected to leverage smart charging

management algorithms to deliver efficient and sustainable charging experiences, minimizing battery degradation and maximizing longevity.

Overall, the OnePlus 12's charging speeds and technology represent the pinnacle of fast charging innovation, offering users rapid and efficient charging experiences that keep pace with their busy lifestyles. Whether it's charging your device in the morning before heading out or topping up during a quick break, Warp Charge technology ensures that you can stay powered up and connected wherever you go.

Battery Optimization Features

Battery optimization features are essential components of a smartphone's software ecosystem, helping users maximize battery life and extend the time between charges. OnePlus devices incorporate a variety of battery optimization features that leverage advanced algorithms and intelligent power management techniques to minimize battery drain and optimize power consumption. With the OnePlus 12, users can expect a comprehensive suite of battery optimization features that ensure efficient and long-lasting battery performance.

Battery Saver Mode:

- Battery Saver Mode is a fundamental feature of OnePlus devices that helps conserve battery life by limiting background processes, reducing screen brightness, and optimizing system performance when the battery level is low.

- The OnePlus 12's Battery Saver Mode may offer customizable settings that allow users to adjust power-saving options according to their preferences, such as activating Battery Saver

Mode automatically when the battery reaches a certain threshold or enabling it manually to extend battery life during extended usage periods.

Adaptive Battery:

- Adaptive Battery is an intelligent battery optimization feature that uses machine learning algorithms to analyze usage patterns and prioritize power for the most frequently used apps and services.
- With Adaptive Battery on the OnePlus 12, users can expect improved battery life

and efficiency as the device learns their usage habits over time and adjusts power allocation accordingly, ensuring that battery power is allocated where it's needed most.

Background App Management:

- Background App Management is a battery optimization feature that restricts the activity of apps running in the background, preventing them from consuming excess battery power and resources.

- The OnePlus 12's background app

management system may include options to manually control which apps are allowed to run in the background and which are restricted, providing users with greater control over battery usage and performance.

Sleep Standby Optimization:

- Sleep Standby Optimization is a feature that intelligently manages background processes and network activity during periods of inactivity, such as when the device is asleep or idle.

- The OnePlus 12's Sleep Standby Optimization may prioritize critical system tasks while reducing non-essential background activity, allowing the device to conserve battery power during periods of extended inactivity without sacrificing performance or functionality.

Screen Optimization:

- Screen Optimization features on the OnePlus 12 help minimize battery drain by adjusting screen brightness, resolution, and refresh rate based on usage patterns and ambient lighting conditions.

- The device may include options to automatically adjust screen brightness and resolution to optimize battery life, as well as manual controls that allow users to fine-tune screen settings according to their preferences and usage scenarios.

App Power Consumption Analysis:

- The OnePlus 12's battery optimization features may include tools for analyzing app power consumption and identifying apps that are draining battery life disproportionately.

- Users can utilize these tools to identify and address apps that are consuming excess battery power, whether through excessive background activity, inefficient resource usage, or other factors, allowing them to optimize battery life and improve overall device performance.

Battery Usage Statistics and Insights:

- OnePlus devices provide detailed battery usage statistics and insights that help users understand how their device's battery is being consumed and identify opportunities for optimization.

- The OnePlus 12's battery usage statistics may include information such as app usage time, battery drain rate, and estimated battery life remaining, empowering users to make informed decisions about their usage habits and battery optimization strategies.

Scheduled Charging:

- Scheduled Charging is a feature that allows users to

optimize battery health and longevity by scheduling charging sessions to occur during off-peak hours or when the device is not in use.

- Users can set up charging schedules for their OnePlus 12 to ensure that the battery is charged gradually and consistently, minimizing stress on the battery cells and prolonging overall battery lifespan.

Overall, the OnePlus 12's battery optimization features are designed to maximize battery life, improve efficiency, and enhance the overall user experience. Whether it's conserving battery power during periods of low usage, optimizing app performance, or extending battery lifespan through intelligent charging management, OnePlus devices empower users to get the most out of their device's battery while minimizing environmental impact.

Chapter Eight: Connectivity Options

5G Connectivity

5G connectivity represents the next generation of mobile network technology, offering faster data speeds, lower latency, and greater network capacity compared to previous generations. With 5G connectivity, users can enjoy enhanced mobile experiences, including smoother streaming, faster downloads, and seamless connectivity for bandwidth-intensive applications. The OnePlus 12 is expected to feature robust 5G connectivity capabilities, enabling users to take advantage of the full potential of 5G networks for a wide range of use cases.

High-Speed Data Transfer:

- 5G connectivity on the OnePlus 12 allows for significantly faster data transfer speeds compared to 4G LTE networks, enabling users to download large files, stream high-definition video, and engage in real-time online activities with minimal lag or buffering.
- With 5G, users can experience download speeds that are several times faster than those

achievable with 4G LTE, making it easier to access and share content on the go without experiencing slowdowns or interruptions.

Low Latency:

- 5G networks offer lower latency compared to previous generations, reducing the delay between sending and receiving data packets and enabling faster response times for real-time applications such as online gaming, video calling, and virtual reality.

- The OnePlus 12's 5G connectivity ensures that

users can enjoy smooth and responsive experiences when interacting with online content and services, whether it's gaming with friends, participating in virtual meetings, or accessing cloud-based applications.

Enhanced Streaming Quality:

- With 5G connectivity, users can enjoy higher-quality streaming experiences, with support for ultra-high-definition (UHD) video streaming, high-fidelity audio streaming, and immersive virtual reality content.

- The OnePlus 12's 5G capabilities enable users to stream high-definition video content seamlessly, without buffering or pixelation, even in congested network environments or areas with limited coverage.

Improved Network Capacity:

- 5G networks have greater network capacity compared to previous generations, allowing for more devices to connect simultaneously and reducing congestion during peak usage times.

- The OnePlus 12's 5G connectivity ensures that users can stay connected and productive even in densely populated areas or crowded venues, where network congestion may otherwise impact performance and reliability.

Future-Proofing:

- Investing in a device with 5G connectivity, such as the OnePlus 12, ensures that users are prepared for the future of mobile connectivity. As 5G networks continue to expand and evolve, users can expect even faster speeds, lower latency, and new innovative applications and services that leverage the full potential of 5G technology.

- By choosing a 5G-enabled device like the OnePlus 12, users can future-proof their investment and ensure that they can take advantage of the latest advancements in mobile connectivity for years to come.

Overall, 5G connectivity on the OnePlus 12 delivers unparalleled speed, performance, and reliability, enabling users to stay connected, productive, and entertained wherever they go. Whether it's streaming high-definition video, playing online games, or accessing cloud-based applications, the OnePlus 12's 5G capabilities ensure that users can enjoy the full potential of 5G networks for a wide range of use cases and applications.

Wi-Fi and Bluetooth

Wi-Fi and Bluetooth are essential wireless connectivity technologies that enable users to connect their devices to the internet and to other compatible devices for data transfer, communication, and multimedia streaming. The OnePlus 12 is expected to feature advanced Wi-Fi and Bluetooth capabilities, providing users with seamless connectivity experiences for a wide range of use cases.

Wi-Fi Connectivity:

- The OnePlus 12 is anticipated to support the latest Wi-Fi standards, including Wi-Fi 6 (802.11ax), which offers faster data speeds, increased network capacity, and improved efficiency compared to previous generations.

- Wi-Fi 6 technology enables the OnePlus 12 to deliver faster internet speeds and more reliable connections, even in congested network environments or areas with multiple connected devices.

- The OnePlus 12 may also feature advanced Wi-Fi optimization features, such as intelligent band steering, beamforming, and MU-MIMO (Multi-User, Multiple Input, Multiple Output), which enhance Wi-Fi performance and coverage throughout the device's operating range.

Bluetooth Connectivity:

- Bluetooth is a wireless communication standard that enables short-range data transfer between devices, such as smartphones, tablets, headphones, speakers, and smartwatches.

- The OnePlus 12 is expected to support the latest Bluetooth standards, including Bluetooth 5.2, which offers improved range, speed, and stability compared to previous versions.

- Bluetooth 5.2 technology enables the OnePlus 12 to deliver faster data transfer speeds, more reliable connections, and greater compatibility with a wide range of Bluetooth-enabled devices.

- The OnePlus 12 may also feature advanced Bluetooth audio codecs, such as aptX, aptX HD, and LDAC, which provide high-quality audio streaming for a superior listening experience when using Bluetooth headphones or speakers.

Dual-Band Wi-Fi and Wi-Fi Hotspot:

- The OnePlus 12 is likely to support dual-band Wi-Fi connectivity, allowing users to connect to both 2.4GHz and 5GHz Wi-Fi networks for optimal performance and compatibility.

- Additionally, the OnePlus 12 may feature Wi-Fi hotspot functionality, enabling users to share their device's internet connection with other devices via Wi-Fi tethering. This feature is useful for creating a portable Wi-Fi network when traveling or when a wired internet connection is not available.

Seamless Connectivity Experience:

- The OnePlus 12's advanced Wi-Fi and Bluetooth capabilities ensure a seamless connectivity experience for users, whether they're streaming high-definition video, playing online games, or transferring files between devices.

- With fast and reliable Wi-Fi and Bluetooth connections, users can enjoy uninterrupted multimedia streaming, crystal-clear voice calls, and smooth data transfer experiences, enhancing productivity and entertainment on the go.

Security and Privacy:

- OnePlus prioritizes security and privacy in its connectivity features, implementing industry-standard encryption protocols and security measures to protect user data and privacy during Wi-Fi and Bluetooth communications.

- The OnePlus 12's Wi-Fi and Bluetooth connectivity features may include options for securing wireless connections with password protection, encryption, and authentication mechanisms, ensuring that user data remains safe and secure when transmitting over wireless networks.

Overall, Wi-Fi and Bluetooth connectivity on the OnePlus 12 provide users with fast, reliable, and secure wireless communication options for a wide range of use cases and applications. Whether it's streaming multimedia content, transferring files between devices, or connecting to wireless accessories, the OnePlus 12's advanced connectivity features ensure that users can stay connected and productive wherever they go.

NFC and Other Connectivity Features

Near Field Communication (NFC) and other connectivity features play a significant role in enabling seamless interactions between devices, facilitating contactless payments, data transfer, and device pairing. The OnePlus 12 is expected to offer a comprehensive range of connectivity features, including NFC, to enhance user convenience and enable a variety of innovative use cases.

Near Field Communication (NFC):

- NFC technology enables short-range wireless communication between devices, allowing for contactless data transfer, payment transactions, and device pairing.
- With NFC on the OnePlus 12, users can enjoy convenient features such as contactless

mobile payments using digital wallet apps, pairing with Bluetooth accessories by tapping compatible devices, and transferring files or information between devices with a simple tap.

Mobile Payments:

- The OnePlus 12's NFC capabilities enable users to make secure mobile payments using supported payment platforms and digital wallet apps.

- With NFC-enabled payment services such as Google Pay or Samsung Pay, users can securely store their credit or debit card information on their device and make contactless payments at NFC-equipped point-of-sale terminals by simply tapping their device.

Device Pairing and Data Transfer:

- NFC simplifies the process of pairing Bluetooth devices by allowing users to initiate device pairing with a simple tap between compatible devices.

- The OnePlus 12's NFC capabilities enable users to quickly pair their device with NFC-enabled Bluetooth accessories, such as headphones, speakers, or smartwatches, without the need for manual Bluetooth pairing procedures.

- Additionally, NFC can be used to transfer files, photos, or contact information between NFC-enabled devices by tapping them together, providing a convenient alternative to traditional data transfer methods such as Bluetooth or Wi-Fi Direct.

Smart Tags and Automation:

- NFC-enabled smart tags, also known as NFC tags or stickers, allow users to automate tasks or trigger actions on their device by tapping it against the tag.

- Users can program NFC tags to perform various actions, such as changing device settings, launching apps, or triggering location-based actions, by writing specific commands or instructions to the tag using a compatible app.

- The OnePlus 12's NFC capabilities enable users to leverage NFC tags for a variety of applications, including home automation, car mode activation, or office productivity tasks, enhancing user convenience and efficiency.

Other Connectivity Features:

- In addition to NFC, the OnePlus 12 may offer a range of other connectivity features to enhance user convenience and enable diverse use cases.

- These features may include Infrared (IR) blaster functionality for controlling home entertainment devices such as TVs and set-top boxes, GPS and navigation support for location-based services, and USB OTG

(On-The-Go) support for connecting external storage devices or accessories to the device via USB.

Future Connectivity Innovations:

- As technology continues to evolve, OnePlus is committed to incorporating new connectivity innovations and features into its devices to enhance user experiences and enable new use cases.

- The OnePlus 12 may introduce new connectivity technologies or enhancements, such as advanced positioning systems, augmented reality

(AR) capabilities, or integration with emerging IoT (Internet of Things) devices and ecosystems, to further expand the device's connectivity capabilities and unlock new possibilities for users.

Overall, NFC and other connectivity features on the OnePlus 12 provide users with versatile and convenient ways to interact with their device, connect with other devices and accessories, and streamline everyday tasks and activities. Whether it's making contactless payments, pairing Bluetooth accessories, or automating tasks with NFC tags, the OnePlus 12's advanced connectivity features ensure that users can stay connected and productive in today's interconnected world.

Chapter Nine: Audio Experience

Speaker Quality

The speaker quality of a smartphone plays a crucial role in delivering an immersive audio experience for multimedia consumption, gaming, and hands-free communication. The OnePlus 12 is anticipated to offer superior speaker quality, providing users with clear, loud, and rich sound output for a variety of use cases.

Dual Stereo Speakers:

- The OnePlus 12 may feature dual stereo speakers, positioned strategically to deliver immersive sound quality with a wide soundstage and spatial audio separation.

- Dual stereo speakers enhance the audio experience by providing balanced sound output across the left and right channels, resulting in more lifelike and engaging audio reproduction for movies, music, and games.

Amplified Sound Output:

- OnePlus devices are known for their amplified sound output, capable of delivering loud and clear audio even in noisy environments.

- The OnePlus 12 is expected to offer enhanced speaker amplification technology, ensuring that users can enjoy crisp and powerful sound without distortion, even at maximum volume levels.

Rich Bass and Clear Highs:

- The speaker system of the OnePlus 12 may be optimized to produce rich bass frequencies and clear high frequencies, providing a balanced audio experience with depth and clarity.
- Whether it's thumping basslines in music tracks or

crisp dialogue in movies, the OnePlus 12's speakers are anticipated to deliver high-fidelity sound reproduction across the entire frequency range.

Dolby Atmos Support:

- OnePlus devices often come with support for advanced audio technologies such as Dolby Atmos, which enhance the audio experience by simulating surround sound effects and spatial audio immersion.
- The OnePlus 12 may feature Dolby Atmos support for its speaker system, allowing

users to enjoy immersive 3D audio experiences with enhanced depth, clarity, and realism for movies, games, and multimedia content.

Call Quality and Speakerphone Performance:

- The speaker quality of the OnePlus 12 extends to voice calls and speakerphone performance, ensuring clear and intelligible audio during phone conversations.

- Advanced noise cancellation algorithms and beamforming microphone technology may be implemented to improve call quality and suppress background noise during speakerphone calls, resulting in crystal-clear voice communication in any environment.

Custom Audio Tuning:

- OnePlus devices often offer customizable audio tuning options that allow users to adjust sound profiles according to their preferences and usage scenarios.

- The OnePlus 12 may come with built-in equalizer settings, audio presets, and customization options that allow users to fine-tune the sound output of the device's speakers to their liking, whether they prefer enhanced bass, vocal clarity, or balanced sound reproduction.

Water and Dust Resistance:

- The OnePlus 12 may feature water and dust resistance ratings that ensure durability and reliability, protecting the device's speaker system from moisture and debris ingress.

- With water and dust resistance, users can confidently use the OnePlus

12's speakers in various environments, including outdoor settings or near water sources, without worrying about damage or performance degradation.

Overall, the speaker quality of the OnePlus 12 is expected to deliver an exceptional audio experience, with immersive sound reproduction, amplified volume levels, and customizable tuning options that cater to a wide range of user preferences and usage scenarios. Whether it's enjoying movies, listening to music, or making hands-free calls, the OnePlus 12's speakers ensure that users can enjoy high-quality audio wherever they go.

Audio Output via Headphone Jack/Bluetooth

The OnePlus 12 is expected to offer versatile audio output options, catering to users who prefer wired headphones connected via the headphone jack or wireless audio devices paired through Bluetooth. Whether it's enjoying music, watching movies, or gaming, the OnePlus 12's audio output capabilities are anticipated to provide high-quality sound experiences tailored to individual preferences.

Headphone Jack Audio Output:

- The OnePlus 12 may feature a headphone jack, allowing users to connect wired headphones or earphones for private listening experiences.

- With the headphone jack, users can enjoy high-fidelity audio output directly from the device, without the need for additional adapters or accessories.

Hi-Fi Audio Support:

- OnePlus devices are known for their support for high-fidelity (Hi-Fi) audio formats, providing audiophiles with superior sound quality and audio detail.

- The OnePlus 12 may offer Hi-Fi audio support through the headphone jack, ensuring that users can enjoy lossless audio playback with enhanced clarity and fidelity.

Dedicated Audio Chipset:

- OnePlus devices often include dedicated audio processing chips or circuitry that enhance audio performance and quality, especially when using wired headphones.
- The OnePlus 12 may feature a dedicated audio chipset that optimizes audio output

for wired headphones, delivering superior sound quality, lower noise levels, and improved dynamic range.

Customizable Audio Settings:

- OnePlus devices typically offer customizable audio settings and equalizer options that allow users to adjust sound profiles according to their preferences.

- The OnePlus 12 may come with built-in equalizer presets, audio tuning options, and customizable settings that enable users to fine-tune the sound output for wired headphones, ensuring an optimized listening experience tailored to individual preferences.

Bluetooth Audio Output:

- In addition to the headphone jack, the OnePlus 12 is expected to support Bluetooth audio output for wireless headphones, earbuds, speakers, and other Bluetooth-enabled audio devices.

- Bluetooth audio on the OnePlus 12 offers the convenience of wireless connectivity, allowing users to enjoy audio playback without the constraints of wired connections.

Advanced Bluetooth Codecs:

- OnePlus devices often support advanced Bluetooth audio codecs such as aptX, aptX HD, LDAC, and AAC, which offer higher-quality audio streaming over Bluetooth connections.

- The OnePlus 12 may feature support for these advanced Bluetooth codecs, ensuring that users can enjoy high-fidelity audio streaming with compatible Bluetooth headphones or speakers.

Low-Latency Bluetooth Audio:

- OnePlus devices may incorporate low-latency Bluetooth audio technology, reducing the delay between audio playback and device output for a more synchronized audiovisual experience.

- Low-latency Bluetooth audio on the OnePlus 12 ensures that users can enjoy seamless audio playback during gaming, video streaming, and other real-time applications without noticeable lag or latency.

Dual Audio Support:

- The OnePlus 12 may support dual audio connectivity, allowing users to pair multiple Bluetooth audio devices simultaneously and share audio output between them.

- Dual audio support enables users to stream audio to multiple Bluetooth speakers or headphones at the same time, creating a synchronized audio experience for group listening or multi-room audio setups.

Overall, the OnePlus 12's audio output capabilities via the headphone jack and Bluetooth offer users a versatile and immersive audio experience, whether they prefer wired or wireless audio solutions. With support for high-fidelity audio formats, customizable audio settings, and advanced Bluetooth connectivity features, the OnePlus 12 ensures that users can enjoy high-quality audio playback tailored to their preferences, wherever they go.

Audio Software Enhancements

The OnePlus 12 is expected to feature advanced audio software enhancements that elevate the overall audio experience for users, delivering immersive sound quality, enhanced customization options, and innovative audio features. These software enhancements leverage cutting-edge technologies and intelligent algorithms to optimize audio performance across various use cases and scenarios.

Audio Enhancement Algorithms:

- The OnePlus 12 may incorporate advanced audio enhancement algorithms that analyze audio signals in real-time and apply digital signal processing techniques to improve sound quality and clarity.

- These enhancement algorithms may include

features such as dynamic range compression, equalization, noise reduction, and spatial audio processing, resulting in a more balanced, immersive, and enjoyable audio experience for users.

Adaptive Sound Profiles:

- OnePlus devices may offer adaptive sound profile settings that automatically adjust audio parameters based on the type of content being played and the user's preferences.

- The OnePlus 12 may feature intelligent audio processing

algorithms that dynamically optimize sound output for different genres of music, movie playback, gaming, and voice calls, ensuring optimal audio quality and clarity across a variety of use cases.

Personalized Audio Calibration:

- The OnePlus 12 may include personalized audio calibration features that allow users to customize sound profiles according to their individual hearing preferences.

- These calibration features may include options for

adjusting audio frequency response, fine-tuning equalizer settings, and optimizing spatial audio characteristics to match the user's unique hearing profile, resulting in a more personalized and immersive listening experience.

Surround Sound Simulation:

- OnePlus devices may offer virtual surround sound simulation features that create a more immersive audio experience for users, simulating the sensation of multi-channel audio playback using stereo speakers or headphones.

- The OnePlus 12 may utilize advanced audio processing algorithms to simulate surround sound effects, enhancing spatial audio perception and immersion during movie playback, gaming, and multimedia consumption.

Intelligent Audio Scene Detection:

- The OnePlus 12 may feature intelligent audio scene detection capabilities that analyze the audio content being played and adjust sound parameters accordingly to optimize the listening experience.

- These scene detection algorithms may automatically identify different types of audio content, such as music, movies, voice calls, or gaming, and apply appropriate audio enhancements and processing techniques to enhance audio quality and clarity for each scenario.

Voice Enhancement and Noise Cancellation:

- OnePlus devices often incorporate voice

enhancement and noise cancellation technologies that improve voice call quality and intelligibility, even in noisy environments.

- The OnePlus 12 may feature advanced voice processing algorithms that suppress background noise, enhance speech clarity, and optimize microphone performance during voice calls, resulting in crystal-clear voice communication experiences for users.

Audio Recording Enhancements:

- The OnePlus 12 may include audio recording

enhancements that improve the quality and clarity of recorded audio, whether it's capturing voice memos, recording videos, or participating in virtual meetings.

- These enhancements may include features such as noise reduction, microphone directionality optimization, and audio post-processing effects, ensuring that recorded audio sounds clear, natural, and professional.

Overall, the OnePlus 12's audio software enhancements are expected to deliver a superior audio experience for users, with immersive sound quality, personalized customization options, and intelligent audio processing features that optimize audio performance across a variety of use cases and scenarios. Whether it's enjoying music, watching movies, playing games, or making voice calls, the OnePlus 12 ensures that users can enjoy high-quality audio playback tailored to their preferences, enhancing their overall multimedia and communication experiences.

Chapter Ten: Security and Privacy Features

Biometric Security Options

Biometric security options provide users with convenient and secure methods for unlocking their devices and protecting sensitive information. The OnePlus 12 is expected to offer a range of biometric security options that cater to different user preferences and security needs, ensuring that users can safeguard their device and personal data with ease.

In-Display Fingerprint Sensor:

- The OnePlus 12 may feature an in-display fingerprint sensor embedded beneath the device's screen, allowing users to unlock their device and authenticate securely with a simple touch.

- In-display fingerprint sensors offer a seamless and intuitive unlocking experience, with fast and reliable fingerprint recognition technology that ensures quick access to the device while maintaining security.

Facial Recognition:

- Facial recognition technology on the OnePlus 12 enables users to unlock their device using facial biometrics, scanning their face to verify identity and grant access to the device.

- The OnePlus 12's facial recognition feature may utilize advanced algorithms and depth-sensing technology to accurately detect and authenticate facial features, providing a convenient and secure biometric authentication method for users.

Biometric Authentication for App Security:

- In addition to unlocking the device, biometric security options on the OnePlus 12 may also be integrated with app security features, allowing users to authenticate access to sensitive apps and data using fingerprint or facial recognition.

- Users can leverage biometric authentication to secure access to confidential apps, banking services, payment platforms, and other sensitive information, adding an extra layer of security beyond traditional password or PIN-based authentication methods.

Multi-Factor Authentication (MFA):

- The OnePlus 12 may support multi-factor authentication (MFA) methods that combine biometric authentication with other security measures, such as PIN codes or pattern locks, to enhance overall device security.

- Users can configure MFA settings to require multiple forms of authentication before granting access to the device or sensitive data, providing an additional layer of protection against unauthorized access or security breaches.

Secure Enclave Technology:

- OnePlus devices often incorporate secure enclave technology, such as TrustZone, to store and process biometric data in a secure and isolated environment, protecting it from unauthorized access or tampering.

- The OnePlus 12's secure enclave technology ensures that biometric data captured by the fingerprint sensor or facial recognition system is encrypted and securely stored within the device, enhancing overall security and privacy protection for users.

Privacy Controls and Data Encryption:

- Biometric security options on the OnePlus 12 may be accompanied by robust privacy controls and data encryption features that safeguard user biometric data and personal information from unauthorized access or misuse.

- Users can take advantage of privacy settings to control how their biometric data is used and shared, ensuring transparency and compliance with privacy regulations such as GDPR (General Data Protection Regulation) and CCPA (California Consumer Privacy Act).

Continuous Security Updates:

- OnePlus is committed to providing regular security updates and patches to address vulnerabilities and enhance device security over time.

- The OnePlus 12 may receive timely security updates that address emerging threats and vulnerabilities, ensuring that biometric security features remain effective and resilient against evolving cybersecurity risks.

Overall, the biometric security options on the OnePlus 12 provide users with convenient and reliable methods for unlocking their device, securing sensitive information, and protecting their privacy. Whether it's using the in-display fingerprint sensor or facial recognition technology, users can enjoy peace of mind knowing that their device and personal data are protected by advanced biometric security features that combine convenience with robust security measures.

Privacy Controls

Privacy controls empower users to manage and protect their personal information, ensuring that sensitive data remains secure and confidential. The OnePlus 12 is expected to offer a comprehensive set of privacy controls, giving users granular control over how their data is accessed, shared, and used by the device and third-party applications.

App Permissions Management:

- The OnePlus 12 may include robust app permissions management features that allow users to control which permissions individual apps have access to.

- Users can review and modify app permissions, such as access to the camera, microphone, location, contacts, and storage, ensuring that apps only access the data they need for their intended functionality.

Fine-Grained Privacy Settings:

- OnePlus devices often offer fine-grained privacy settings that allow users to customize privacy preferences according to their preferences and security needs.

- The OnePlus 12 may feature options to restrict background app activity, disable ad personalization, limit app tracking, and prevent apps from collecting data in the background, enhancing overall privacy protection for users.

Private Safe and File Encryption:

- The OnePlus 12 may include a Private Safe feature that allows users to securely store sensitive files, photos, and documents in an encrypted vault protected by a PIN, password, or biometric authentication.

- Private Safe ensures that confidential data remains secure and inaccessible to unauthorized users, providing an additional layer of protection against data breaches or unauthorized access.

Secure Lock Screen Options:

- OnePlus devices offer secure lock screen options, such as PIN codes, pattern locks, and biometric authentication methods, to prevent unauthorized access

to the device and personal
data.

- The OnePlus 12 may feature
advanced lock screen
customization options that
allow users to choose their
preferred lock screen
method and set up
additional security
measures, such as
automatic lock timers and
lock screen message
customization.

Data Encryption and Secure
Storage:

- The OnePlus 12 may utilize
data encryption and secure
storage technologies to

protect user data stored on the device, including photos, videos, messages, and app data.

- Data encryption ensures that sensitive information is encrypted and stored securely on the device's internal storage, making it unreadable to unauthorized parties even if the device is lost or stolen.

Privacy-Focused Browser and Search Engine:

- OnePlus devices may offer a privacy-focused web browser and search engine that prioritize user privacy and data protection.

- The OnePlus 12 may feature a built-in browser with privacy-enhancing features such as ad blocking, tracker blocking, and enhanced privacy modes that prevent websites from tracking user activity or collecting personal information.

Anonymous Usage Statistics and Telemetry:

- OnePlus respects user privacy by offering options to opt-out of anonymous usage statistics and telemetry data collection.

- The OnePlus 12 may include settings that allow users to control whether anonymous usage statistics and diagnostic data are sent to OnePlus for analysis, ensuring transparency and giving users control over their data.

Regular Privacy Audits and Transparency Reports:

- OnePlus is committed to transparency and accountability in its privacy practices, conducting regular privacy audits and publishing transparency reports to disclose how user data is collected, used, and protected.

- Users can access privacy policies, terms of service agreements, and transparency reports to understand OnePlus' privacy practices and make informed decisions about their privacy and data security.

Overall, privacy controls on the OnePlus 12 empower users to take control of their personal information and protect their privacy in an increasingly connected world. With features such as app permissions management, data encryption, and privacy-focused browsing options, users can enjoy peace of mind knowing that their data is secure and confidential on their OnePlus 12 device.

Encryption and Secure Features

Encryption and secure features are essential components of modern smartphones, providing robust protection for user data against unauthorized access and cyber threats. The OnePlus 12 is expected to integrate advanced encryption and secure features to safeguard sensitive information and enhance overall device security.

Data Encryption:

- The OnePlus 12 is anticipated to utilize data encryption technology to protect user data stored on the device's internal storage and external storage media.

- Data encryption converts user data into an unreadable format using encryption algorithms, making it inaccessible to unauthorized parties without the encryption key.

File-Based Encryption (FBE):

- OnePlus devices may implement file-based encryption (FBE), which encrypts individual files and directories on the device, providing granular protection for user data.

- FBE ensures that each file is encrypted separately, allowing for efficient management of encrypted data and minimizing performance overhead.

Secure Boot and Trusted Boot:

- The OnePlus 12 may feature secure boot and trusted boot mechanisms that ensure the integrity of the device's operating system and firmware during startup.
- Secure boot verifies the authenticity and integrity of

the bootloader and operating system components, preventing unauthorized modifications or tampering that could compromise device security.

Hardware-Level Security:

- OnePlus devices often incorporate hardware-level security features, such as dedicated security chips and secure elements, to protect sensitive data and cryptographic keys.
- Hardware-level security ensures that critical security functions, such as biometric authentication and

cryptographic operations, are performed in a secure and isolated environment, mitigating the risk of unauthorized access or tampering.

Secure Enclave Technology:

- The OnePlus 12 may utilize secure enclave technology, such as TrustZone, to store and process sensitive information, including biometric data and cryptographic keys, in a secure and isolated environment.

- Secure enclave technology protects sensitive data from

unauthorized access or extraction by malicious actors, ensuring that user privacy and security are maintained even in the event of a security breach.

Hardware-Based Encryption Acceleration:

- OnePlus devices may feature hardware-based encryption acceleration capabilities that optimize the performance of encryption and decryption operations, minimizing the impact on device performance and battery life.

- Hardware-based encryption acceleration ensures that data encryption and decryption processes are performed efficiently and securely, without compromising user experience or device responsiveness.

Secure Communication Protocols:

- The OnePlus 12 may support secure communication protocols, such as TLS (Transport Layer Security) and VPN (Virtual Private Network), to encrypt data transmitted over networks and protect it from interception or eavesdropping.

- Secure communication protocols ensure that sensitive information, such as passwords, financial transactions, and personal communications, remains confidential and secure during transmission over the internet or cellular networks.

Biometric Authentication:

- Biometric authentication methods, such as fingerprint recognition and facial recognition, provide secure and convenient ways for users to unlock their device and authenticate securely.

- The OnePlus 12 may offer advanced biometric authentication features that leverage hardware-level security and encryption to protect biometric data and ensure secure authentication processes.

Regular Security Updates:

- OnePlus is committed to providing regular security updates and patches to address vulnerabilities and security risks, ensuring that the OnePlus 12 remains protected against emerging threats and attacks.

- Regular security updates enhance device security by patching known vulnerabilities, improving system stability, and addressing potential security weaknesses in the device's software and firmware.

Overall, encryption and secure features on the OnePlus 12 provide users with robust protection for their data and enhance overall device security against unauthorized access, cyber threats, and data breaches. By leveraging advanced encryption technology, hardware-level security features, and regular security updates, the OnePlus 12 ensures that user data remains secure and confidential, even in the face of evolving cybersecurity risks and challenges.

Chapter Eleven: Accessories and Additional Features

Official Accessories

OnePlus offers a range of official accessories designed to complement and enhance the functionality of their smartphones, including the OnePlus 12. These accessories are crafted with attention to detail and precision engineering, ensuring compatibility, durability, and seamless integration with the OnePlus ecosystem. Here are some of the official accessories that users can expect for the OnePlus 12:

OnePlus Buds:

- OnePlus Buds are wireless earbuds designed to deliver high-quality audio and seamless connectivity with OnePlus smartphones, including the OnePlus 12.
- With features such as Bluetooth 5.0 connectivity, low-latency gaming mode, and long-lasting battery life, OnePlus Buds provide users with an immersive and reliable audio experience for

music playback, gaming, and hands-free communication.

OnePlus Warp Charge Accessories:

- OnePlus Warp Charge accessories, including Warp Charge 65 Power Adapter and Warp Charge 50 Wireless Charger, offer fast and efficient charging solutions for the OnePlus 12.

- Warp Charge technology delivers ultra-fast charging speeds, allowing users to quickly recharge their device's battery and minimize downtime. Whether it's wired or wireless charging, OnePlus Warp Charge accessories ensure that users can stay powered up and ready to go.

OnePlus Cases and Covers:

- OnePlus offers a variety of cases and covers designed to protect and personalize the OnePlus 12 while maintaining its sleek and stylish design.

- From rugged protective cases to slim and lightweight covers, OnePlus cases provide users with options to suit their preferences and lifestyle. Features such as shock absorption, raised edges, and precise cutouts ensure that the OnePlus 12 remains safe from scratches, bumps, and accidental drops.

OnePlus Screen Protectors:

- OnePlus screen protectors offer an additional layer of defense for the OnePlus 12's display, safeguarding it against scratches, smudges, and minor impacts.

- Made from high-quality tempered glass or film materials, OnePlus screen protectors provide crystal-clear visibility and responsive touch sensitivity, ensuring that users can enjoy a pristine viewing experience while keeping their device's display protected.

OnePlus Charging Cables and Adapters:

- OnePlus offers a range of charging cables and adapters designed for use with the OnePlus 12, ensuring compatibility and optimal charging performance.

- Whether it's USB Type-C cables, wall chargers, or car chargers, OnePlus charging accessories provide users with reliable and efficient charging solutions for their devices, whether at home, in the office, or on the go.

OnePlus Wireless Earphones and Headphones:

- In addition to OnePlus Buds, OnePlus offers a selection of wireless earphones and headphones that provide users with premium audio quality and comfort.

- From true wireless earphones to over-ear headphones, OnePlus wireless audio accessories feature advanced sound technology, ergonomic designs, and long-lasting battery life, offering users an immersive listening experience for music, movies, and gaming.

OnePlus Gaming Accessories:

- OnePlus gaming accessories, such as the OnePlus Gaming Triggers and OnePlus Gaming Backpack, are designed to enhance the gaming experience on the OnePlus 12.

- Gaming Triggers provide tactile feedback and precise control for mobile gaming, while the Gaming Backpack

offers storage space for the
OnePlus 12, accessories,
and gaming peripherals,
ensuring that users can
game on the go with comfort
and convenience.

OnePlus Smartwatch and Fitness
Bands:

- Rumors suggest that
  OnePlus may introduce a
  smartwatch or fitness bands
  as official accessories for
  the OnePlus 12, providing
  users with wearable
  technology solutions for
  health tracking, notifications,
  and connectivity.

- With features such as heart rate monitoring, activity tracking, and smartphone integration, OnePlus smartwatches and fitness bands offer users a convenient and stylish way to stay connected and motivated to achieve their fitness goals.

Overall, OnePlus' official accessories for the OnePlus 12 are designed to complement the device's features and enhance the user experience, offering users a range of options to personalize, protect, and optimize their device according to their preferences and lifestyle. From audio accessories and charging solutions to protective cases and gaming peripherals, OnePlus accessories provide users with everything they need to get the most out of their OnePlus 12 smartphone.

Third-Party Compatible Accessories

In addition to OnePlus' official accessories, users can also explore a wide range of third-party accessories that are compatible with the OnePlus 12. These accessories, offered by various manufacturers and brands, cater to different user preferences and needs, providing additional options for personalization, protection, and functionality. Here are some examples of third-party compatible accessories for the OnePlus 12:

Protective Cases and Covers:

- Third-party manufacturers offer a diverse selection of protective cases and covers for the OnePlus 12, providing users with options beyond OnePlus' official offerings.

- From rugged cases with heavy-duty protection to slim and stylish covers with unique designs, third-party protective accessories allow users to customize the look and feel of their device while ensuring reliable protection against scratches, bumps, and drops.

Screen Protectors:

- Screen protectors from third-party manufacturers are available in various materials, including tempered glass and film, providing users with options to safeguard the OnePlus 12's display against scratches, smudges, and cracks.

- These screen protectors offer features such as anti-fingerprint coatings, bubble-free installation, and precise cutouts, ensuring that users can enjoy a clear and responsive touchscreen experience while keeping their device's display protected.

Charging Cables and Adapters:

- Third-party charging cables and adapters compatible with the OnePlus 12 offer alternative charging solutions for users who prefer additional length, durability, or convenience.

- Whether it's braided USB Type-C cables, multi-port wall chargers, or car chargers with fast-charging capabilities, third-party charging accessories provide users with versatile and reliable charging options for their OnePlus 12 devices.

Wireless Chargers and Charging Pads:

- Third-party wireless chargers and charging pads compatible with the OnePlus 12 offer wireless charging solutions that are compatible with Qi-enabled devices.

- These wireless charging accessories come in various designs and form factors, including flat charging pads, vertical stands, and multi-device charging stations, allowing users to charge their OnePlus 12 wirelessly with ease and convenience.

Car Mounts and Holders:

- Car mounts and holders designed for the OnePlus 12 provide users with secure and convenient mounting solutions for use in vehicles.

- Whether it's dashboard mounts, air vent mounts, or windshield mounts, third-party car accessories offer adjustable viewing angles, secure grip, and easy installation, ensuring that users can safely use their OnePlus 12 for navigation, hands-free calling, and multimedia playback while on the road.

Bluetooth Earphones and Headphones:

- Third-party Bluetooth earphones and headphones offer users alternative options for wireless audio playback and hands-free communication with the OnePlus 12.

- From true wireless earbuds to over-ear headphones, third-party audio accessories feature advanced sound technology, ergonomic designs, and long-lasting battery life, providing users with an immersive listening experience for music, movies, and calls.

Portable Power Banks:

- Portable power banks from third-party manufacturers offer users additional power backup for charging their OnePlus 12 devices on the go.
- These power banks come in various capacities, sizes, and designs, allowing users to choose the right power

bank that suits their needs and preferences for extended battery life and mobile charging convenience.

Camera Lenses and Accessories:

- Camera lenses and accessories compatible with the OnePlus 12 provide users with options to enhance their photography and videography capabilities.

- From wide-angle lenses and macro lenses to lens attachments and filters, third-party camera accessories offer creative options for capturing stunning photos and videos with the OnePlus 12's camera system.

Overall, third-party compatible accessories for the OnePlus 12 expand the range of options available to users, providing additional choices for personalization, protection, and functionality. Whether it's protective cases, charging solutions, audio accessories, or camera enhancements, third-party accessories offer users the flexibility to customize their OnePlus 12 experience according to their preferences and needs.

Unique Features and Offerings

The OnePlus 12 is anticipated to introduce several unique features and offerings that set it apart from other smartphones in the market. These features are designed to enhance user experience, functionality, and convenience, making the OnePlus 12 an attractive choice for consumers. Here are some of the unique features and offerings expected with the OnePlus 12:

HyperBoost Performance Optimization:

- The OnePlus 12 may introduce HyperBoost, an advanced performance optimization technology that enhances system performance, gaming experience, and app responsiveness.

- HyperBoost utilizes intelligent algorithms and system-level optimizations to allocate resources efficiently, reduce latency, and minimize frame drops during gaming and multitasking, ensuring smooth and lag-free performance for users.

AI-Powered Camera Enhancements:

- OnePlus 12's camera system may feature AI-powered

enhancements that optimize photo and video quality, scene recognition, and image processing capabilities.

- AI algorithms analyze scenes in real-time, adjust camera settings, and apply post-processing effects to enhance image clarity, color accuracy, and dynamic range, resulting in stunning photos and videos captured with the OnePlus 12.

Adaptive Refresh Rate Display:

- The OnePlus 12 may introduce an adaptive refresh rate display technology that dynamically adjusts the screen refresh rate based on content and usage scenarios.

- By intelligently scaling refresh rates between 60Hz and 120Hz, the adaptive display optimizes power efficiency, reduces screen flicker, and enhances visual fluidity for tasks such as scrolling, gaming, and video playback, providing a smoother and more responsive user experience.

Enhanced OxygenOS with AI Assistant:

- OxygenOS on the OnePlus 12 may feature an enhanced user interface with integrated AI assistant capabilities, providing users with personalized recommendations, proactive notifications, and intelligent assistance.

- The AI assistant learns user preferences, habits, and usage patterns to anticipate user needs, offer contextual suggestions, and automate routine tasks, streamlining user interactions and enhancing productivity.

Ultrasonic Under-Display Touch ID:

- The OnePlus 12 may incorporate ultrasonic under-display touch ID technology that offers faster and more secure fingerprint recognition compared to traditional optical sensors.
- Ultrasonic touch ID sensors use ultrasonic waves to create a 3D map of the user's fingerprint, providing greater accuracy, reliability, and resistance to spoofing attacks, ensuring that user data remains protected and accessible with a quick and secure fingerprint scan.

Dynamic Haptic Feedback Engine:

- OnePlus 12's haptic feedback system may feature a dynamic haptic feedback engine that provides precise and immersive tactile feedback for user interactions.

- The dynamic haptic feedback engine utilizes advanced vibration motors and intelligent algorithms to simulate realistic sensations, such as clicks, taps, and vibrations, enhancing the user experience for typing, gaming, and interacting with the device's touchscreen.

Wireless Audio Sharing Technology:

- The OnePlus 12 may introduce wireless audio sharing technology that allows users to share audio wirelessly with compatible Bluetooth devices, such as headphones, earbuds, and speakers.

- Wireless audio sharing enables users to stream audio simultaneously to multiple Bluetooth devices, creating a shared listening experience for group activities, movie nights, and gaming sessions, without the need for wired connections or additional accessories.

Enhanced Privacy and Security Features:

- OnePlus 12 may offer enhanced privacy and security features, such as app sandboxing, secure folder encryption, and privacy-focused browsing modes, to protect user data and ensure confidentiality.

- These features empower users to control their digital footprint, manage app permissions, and safeguard sensitive information from unauthorized access or data breaches, ensuring peace of mind and privacy protection in an increasingly connected world.

Overall, the OnePlus 12's unique features and offerings are designed to elevate the user experience, deliver innovative functionality, and provide users with greater control, convenience, and security in their day-to-day interactions with the device. Whether it's AI-powered camera enhancements, adaptive display technology, or dynamic haptic feedback, the OnePlus 12 sets a new standard for smartphone innovation and user-centric design, making it a compelling choice for tech enthusiasts and smartphone users alike.

Chapter Twelve: User Tips and Tricks

Optimizing Battery Life

Battery life is a critical aspect of smartphone usage, and optimizing it can significantly enhance the overall user experience. Here are some tips and tricks to optimize battery life on the OnePlus 12:

Adjust Screen Brightness:

- Lowering the screen brightness can significantly reduce battery consumption. Use the adaptive brightness feature or manually adjust the brightness level based on ambient lighting conditions.

Enable Battery Saver Mode:

- OnePlus devices offer a Battery Saver mode that reduces background activities, limits performance, and adjusts system settings to conserve battery life. Enable Battery Saver mode when the battery is low or when you need to extend usage time.

Manage App Permissions:

- Review and manage app permissions to prevent unnecessary background activities and reduce battery drain. Restrict apps from accessing location, camera, and other sensitive features unless required.

Optimize App Settings:

- Some apps may consume more battery due to inefficient settings or background activities. Review app settings and disable features like background refresh, location tracking, and notifications for apps that you don't frequently use.

Use Dark Mode:

- Dark mode reduces power consumption on devices

with OLED displays by displaying dark backgrounds instead of bright ones. Enable dark mode in system settings or within compatible apps to save battery power, especially on the OnePlus 12's AMOLED display.

Manage Connectivity Options:

- Disable Wi-Fi, Bluetooth, and GPS when not in use to prevent unnecessary battery drain. Additionally, consider using airplane mode in areas with poor network coverage to conserve battery power.

Limit Background Syncing:

- Reduce the frequency of background syncing for emails, social media, and other apps to minimize data usage and battery drain. Manually sync apps when needed or adjust sync intervals in app settings.

Monitor Battery Usage:

- Use the built-in battery usage monitor in OxygenOS to identify apps and services consuming the most battery power. Address any abnormal battery drain by troubleshooting or uninstalling problematic apps.

Update Software Regularly:

- Keep the OnePlus 12's software up to date with the latest firmware updates and security patches. Software updates often include optimizations and fixes that can improve battery performance and overall device efficiency.

Use Battery Optimization Features:

- Take advantage of battery optimization features in OxygenOS to manage power-hungry apps and optimize system performance. Enable Battery Optimization in settings to prioritize battery life and extend usage time.

Charge Wisely:

- Avoid frequent full discharges and charging the battery to 100% capacity regularly. Instead, aim for shallow discharge cycles and charge the battery to around 80% for optimal battery health and longevity.

Use Battery-Friendly Accessories:

- Invest in certified chargers and cables that are compatible with OnePlus devices to ensure safe and efficient charging. Low-quality or counterfeit accessories may damage the battery and compromise performance.

By implementing these tips and tricks, users can effectively optimize battery life on the OnePlus 12, ensuring longer usage time, improved efficiency, and a better overall smartphone experience.

Customization Tips

Customization is a hallmark of OnePlus devices, allowing users to personalize their experience and tailor the device to their preferences. Here are some tips and tricks for customizing your OnePlus 12:

Theme Store and Customization Options:

- Explore the Theme Store in OxygenOS to discover a variety of themes, wallpapers, and icon packs that can transform the look and feel of your device. Customize your home screen, lock screen, and system interface with themes that reflect your style.

Customize Home Screen Layout:

- Long-press on the home screen to access customization options such as changing wallpapers, adding widgets, and adjusting icon layouts. Experiment with different home screen layouts to optimize organization and accessibility.

Gesture Navigation and Navigation Bar:

- Customize navigation gestures and the navigation bar to streamline navigation and multitasking. Enable gestures for tasks like back, home, and recent apps, or customize the navigation bar layout to suit your preferences.

App Drawer and Icon Packs:

- Customize the app drawer layout and organization by categorizing apps into folders, hiding unused apps, or rearranging app icons. Additionally, install icon packs from the Play Store to give your app icons a fresh new look.

Customize Status Bar and Quick Settings:

- Tailor the status bar and quick settings panel by choosing which icons to display, rearranging quick settings tiles, and adjusting display preferences. Customize the status bar with battery percentage, network indicators, and notification icons.

Customizable Alert Slider:

- Take advantage of the Alert Slider on the side of the device to customize notification preferences and profiles. Configure the Alert Slider to toggle between silent, vibrate, and ring modes based on your preferences and usage scenarios.

Lock Screen Customization:

- Customize the lock screen with personalized wallpapers, clock styles, and notification settings. Enable lock screen shortcuts for quick access to frequently used apps or actions without unlocking the device.

OnePlus Shelf and Widgets:

- Customize the OnePlus Shelf by adding widgets, memos, and recent contacts for quick access to important information and shortcuts. Personalize the Shelf layout and content to suit your workflow and productivity needs.

Create Custom Themes and Presets:

- Use the built-in Theme Customization tool in OxygenOS to create custom themes and presets that reflect your unique style and preferences. Customize system fonts, accent colors, and icon shapes to create a theme that's uniquely yours.

Use Third-Party Customization Apps:

- Explore third-party customization apps and launchers available on the Play Store to further personalize your OnePlus 12. Experiment with different launchers, widgets, and customization tools to create a setup that suits your taste.

Backup and Restore Customizations:

- Backup your customization settings, themes, and preferences to ensure seamless transition between devices or after a factory reset. Use OnePlus Switch or third-party backup apps to save and restore your customization settings effortlessly.

By leveraging these customization tips and tricks, users can unlock the full potential of their OnePlus 12 and create a personalized experience that reflects their individual style, preferences, and workflow. Whether it's customizing the home screen, tweaking navigation settings, or creating custom themes, OnePlus devices offer extensive customization options that empower users to make their device truly their own.

Camera Tips and Tricks

The camera system of the OnePlus 12 is expected to be a standout feature, offering advanced capabilities for capturing stunning photos and videos. Here are some tips and tricks to help you make the most of your OnePlus 12's camera:

Understand Camera Modes and Settings:

- Familiarize yourself with the various camera modes and settings available on the OnePlus 12, including Auto mode, Pro mode, Nightscape, Portrait mode, and more. Experiment with different modes to understand their features and capabilities.

Use Pro Mode for Manual Control:

- Pro mode allows you to manually adjust settings such as ISO, shutter speed, white balance, and focus, giving you greater control over your shots. Use Pro mode in situations where you want precise control over exposure and image quality.

Experiment with Different Lenses:

- The OnePlus 12 is expected to feature multiple camera lenses, including wide-angle, ultra-wide, and telephoto lenses. Experiment with different lenses to capture unique perspectives and compositions.

Master Portrait Mode for Portraits:

- Portrait mode on the OnePlus 12 is designed to blur the background and highlight the subject, creating professional-looking portraits. Ensure proper lighting and composition when using Portrait mode for optimal results.

Utilize Nightscape Mode for Low-Light Shots:

- Nightscape mode enhances low-light photography by capturing multiple exposures and combining them to reduce noise and improve detail in dark scenes. Use Nightscape mode in low-light conditions for brighter and clearer night shots.

Enable AI Scene Detection for Automatic Optimization:

- OnePlus devices often feature AI scene detection technology that automatically identifies scenes and adjusts camera settings for optimal results. Enable AI scene detection to let the camera intelligently optimize settings based on the scene you're capturing.

Tap to Focus and Adjust Exposure:

- Tap on the screen to manually adjust the focus point and exposure in the camera viewfinder. This allows you to control which part of the scene is in focus and ensure proper exposure for your shots.

Use Gridlines for Composition:

- Enable gridlines in the camera settings to help you compose better shots using the rule of thirds or other composition techniques. Align key elements of your scene with the gridlines for balanced and visually appealing photos.

Capture Raw Images for Post-Processing:

- If you're into post-processing your photos, consider capturing raw images (if supported) in Pro mode. Raw images contain unprocessed data from the camera sensor, allowing for more flexibility and control during editing.

Experiment with Panorama and Time-Lapse Modes:

- Explore the Panorama and Time-Lapse modes on the OnePlus 12 to capture breathtaking panoramic views and creative time-lapse sequences. These modes offer unique ways to capture dynamic scenes and add variety to your photography.

Practice Stability and Composition Techniques:

- Use stabilization techniques such as bracing your arms against your body or using a tripod to minimize camera shake and ensure sharp images. Additionally, pay attention to composition principles such as leading lines, symmetry, and framing to create compelling photos.

Edit and Share Your Photos:

- Take advantage of built-in editing tools or third-party

photo editing apps to enhance and fine-tune your photos before sharing them. Experiment with adjustments such as exposure, contrast, saturation, and cropping to achieve your desired look.

By incorporating these camera tips and tricks into your photography workflow, you can unlock the full potential of the OnePlus 12's camera system and capture stunning photos and videos in a variety of shooting conditions. Whether you're a photography enthusiast or a casual shooter, these tips will help you take your mobile photography to the next level.

Chapter Thirteen: Troubleshooting and FAQs

Common Issues and Solutions

Despite being well-designed and optimized, the OnePlus 12 may encounter occasional issues that can affect user experience. Here are some common issues and their potential solutions:

Battery Drain:

- Issue: The device's battery drains faster than expected, even with normal usage.
- Solution:
    - Check battery usage statistics in settings to

identify apps consuming excessive power and optimize their settings.

- Enable Battery Saver mode to limit background activities and extend battery life.
- Ensure that the device is running the latest software updates, as they may include optimizations for battery performance.

Overheating:

- Issue: The device becomes excessively hot during

prolonged usage or while charging.

- Solution:
    - Avoid using the device in direct sunlight or in hot environments for extended periods.
    - Close background apps and reduce screen brightness to minimize heat generation.
    - If overheating occurs during charging, ensure that the charger and cable are compatible and in good condition.

Connectivity Issues:

- Issue: Wi-Fi, Bluetooth, or cellular connectivity is unstable or not working.
- Solution:
    - Toggle airplane mode on and off to reset network connections.
    - Forget and re-add Wi-Fi networks or Bluetooth devices to troubleshoot connection issues.
    - Ensure that the device is within range of the Wi-Fi router or Bluetooth device and

that they are functioning properly.

Performance Lag or Freezing:

- Issue: The device experiences performance lag, stuttering, or freezing during usage.

- Solution:

    - Close background apps and clear cached data to free up system resources.

    - Restart the device to refresh system processes and clear temporary files.

    - If performance issues persist, consider

performing a factory reset after backing up important data.

Camera Problems:

- Issue: The camera app crashes, fails to focus, or produces poor-quality photos/videos.

- Solution:

    - Force close the camera app and restart it to see if the issue resolves.

    - Clear the camera app's cache and data in settings to reset its settings and preferences.

- Ensure that the camera lens is clean and free from obstruction, and that there are no software conflicts causing the issue.

Software Glitches:

- Issue: Random software glitches or bugs occur, affecting device stability and performance.
- Solution:
    - Check for and install any available software updates, as they may include bug fixes and stability improvements.

- If specific apps are causing issues, try updating or reinstalling them to see if the problem resolves.

- Consider performing a factory reset as a last resort to reset the device to its default settings and resolve persistent software issues.

Touchscreen Sensitivity Problems:

- Issue: The touchscreen is unresponsive or experiences erratic behavior.

- Solution:

- Clean the touchscreen with a soft, lint-free cloth to remove any dirt or debris that may be affecting responsiveness.
- Ensure that the device's screen protector is properly aligned and not interfering with touchscreen sensitivity.
- If touchscreen issues persist, consider recalibrating the touchscreen in settings or contacting

OnePlus support for further assistance.

Biometric Authentication Issues:

- Issue: Fingerprint or facial recognition authentication fails or becomes unreliable.
- Solution:
    - Re-register fingerprints or facial data to ensure accurate recognition.
    - Clean the fingerprint sensor or front-facing camera lens to remove any dirt or smudges that may affect recognition.
    - If biometric authentication issues

persist, consider resetting biometric data or contacting OnePlus support for assistance.

By following these troubleshooting steps and solutions, users can address common issues and maintain optimal performance with their OnePlus 12 device. If problems persist despite troubleshooting efforts, consider reaching out to OnePlus customer support for further assistance and guidance.

Frequently Asked Questions

Here are some frequently asked questions (FAQs) about the OnePlus 12:

When will the OnePlus 12 be released?

- The release date for the OnePlus 12 has not been officially announced. Stay tuned for updates from OnePlus regarding the launch schedule.

What are the key features of the OnePlus 12?

- While specific features of the OnePlus 12 have not been confirmed, it is anticipated to offer advancements in camera technology, performance, display quality, and software experience, building upon the strengths of previous OnePlus models.

Will the OnePlus 12 support 5G connectivity?

- Given the industry trend towards 5G technology, it's likely that the OnePlus 12 will support 5G connectivity to deliver faster download/upload speeds and improved network performance.

What will be the battery capacity of the OnePlus 12?

- The battery capacity of the OnePlus 12 has not been officially disclosed. However, OnePlus typically equips its flagship devices with batteries that offer long-lasting usage and fast charging capabilities.

Will the OnePlus 12 feature wireless charging?

- While OnePlus has previously included wireless charging in some of its devices, it's uncertain whether the OnePlus 12 will have this feature. Stay updated for official announcements from OnePlus regarding the specifications of the OnePlus 12.

What will be the price range of the OnePlus 12?

- Pricing details for the OnePlus 12 have not been confirmed. The final price will likely depend on factors such as the device's specifications, features, and market competition.

Will the OnePlus 12 come with a headphone jack?

- OnePlus has gradually phased out the headphone jack from its flagship devices in recent years. It's uncertain whether the OnePlus 12 will include a headphone jack or rely solely on USB Type-C or wireless audio connectivity.

What software will the OnePlus 12 run on?

- The OnePlus 12 is expected to run on OxygenOS, OnePlus' custom Android-based operating system. OxygenOS offers a clean and customizable user experience with additional features and optimizations.

Will the OnePlus 12 have expandable storage?

- OnePlus devices typically do not support expandable storage via microSD cards. Users can choose from different storage configurations offered by OnePlus when purchasing the device.

Is the OnePlus 12 waterproof or water-resistant?

- OnePlus devices have featured varying levels of water resistance in the past. It's recommended to check the official specifications and IP rating of the OnePlus 12 for information on its water resistance capabilities.

Will the OnePlus 12 have a high refresh rate display?

- OnePlus has been known for incorporating high refresh rate displays in its flagship devices. It's likely that the OnePlus 12 will feature a high refresh rate display for smoother scrolling and improved gaming experience.

Can I use 4G SIM cards with the OnePlus 12?

- Yes, the OnePlus 12 is expected to support 4G SIM cards in addition to 5G connectivity, providing compatibility with existing networks and ensuring seamless connectivity for users.

These FAQs provide answers to common inquiries about the OnePlus 12. As more information becomes available, OnePlus will likely address additional questions and concerns from consumers regarding the device's specifications, features, and availability. Stay tuned for official announcements and updates from OnePlus regarding the OnePlus 12.

Conclusion

After diving deep into the OnePlus 12 and exploring its myriad features, specifications, and capabilities, it's clear that this device embodies the spirit of innovation and excellence that OnePlus is known for. Let's recap some of the key features of the OnePlus 12 and conclude with final thoughts and recommendations.

Recap of OnePlus 12 Features

The OnePlus 12 is a flagship smartphone that pushes the boundaries of technology and user experience. Here's a recap of its standout features:

Cutting-Edge Camera System: The OnePlus 12 boasts an advanced camera system with multiple lenses, AI-powered enhancements, and innovative features for capturing stunning photos and videos in any scenario.

Powerful Performance: Equipped with a high-performance processor, ample RAM, and fast storage options, the OnePlus 12 delivers smooth multitasking, lag-free gaming, and swift app launches for an unparalleled user experience.

Immersive Display: The OnePlus 12 features a vibrant and immersive display with high refresh rates, HDR support, and accurate color reproduction, providing an exceptional viewing experience for multimedia content and gaming.

Long-Lasting Battery: With a large battery capacity and efficient power management features, the OnePlus 12 offers long-lasting battery life and fast charging capabilities, ensuring uninterrupted usage throughout the day.

Customizable Software: Running on OxygenOS, the OnePlus 12 offers a clean, customizable, and feature-rich user interface with a wealth of customization options, productivity tools, and optimization features to tailor the device to your preferences.

Premium Design and Build Quality: Crafted from premium materials and featuring a sleek and ergonomic design, the OnePlus 12 exudes sophistication and durability, making it a pleasure to hold and use.

Final Thoughts and Recommendations

In conclusion, the OnePlus 12 represents the pinnacle of smartphone innovation, combining cutting-edge technology, exceptional performance, and thoughtful design to deliver an unmatched user experience. Whether you're a photography enthusiast, a power user, or someone who values style and reliability, the OnePlus 12 is sure to impress with its feature-packed design and impeccable craftsmanship.

As a recommendation, we highly encourage users to explore the OnePlus 12's features, experiment with its customization options, and unleash its full potential to suit their individual needs and preferences. With its blend of performance, style, and innovation, the OnePlus 12 is more than just a smartphone—it's a companion that empowers you to do more, capture more, and experience more in every aspect of your digital life.

In a rapidly evolving smartphone landscape, OnePlus continues to set the standard for excellence and innovation, and the OnePlus 12 is a shining example of the brand's commitment to pushing boundaries and exceeding expectations. Whether you're upgrading from a previous OnePlus device or considering your first OnePlus smartphone, the OnePlus 12 is undoubtedly a device worth considering for its unparalleled features, performance, and value.

With that, we conclude our in-depth review and user guide of the OnePlus 12. Thank you for joining us on this journey, and we look forward to seeing how the OnePlus 12 enhances your

mobile experience and inspires you to
do more.

Appendices

Glossary of Terms

To assist users in understanding technical terms and jargon used throughout the OnePlus 12 review and user guide, here's a glossary of common terms:

- AMOLED: Active Matrix Organic Light Emitting Diode, a display technology known for its vibrant colors, high contrast ratios, and energy efficiency.
- CPU: Central Processing Unit, the primary component responsible for executing instructions and performing calculations in a computer or smartphone.

- GPU: Graphics Processing Unit, a specialized processor designed to handle graphics-related tasks such as rendering images, videos, and 3D graphics.

- HDR: High Dynamic Range, a display technology that enhances contrast and color accuracy by expanding the range of luminance levels displayed.

- mAh: Milliampere-hour, a unit of measure for electrical charge commonly used to specify the capacity of a battery.

- NFC: Near Field Communication, a wireless communication technology that enables short-range data exchange between devices.

- OLED: Organic Light Emitting Diode, a display technology that uses organic compounds to emit light and create images on the screen.
- RAM: Random Access Memory, a type of computer memory that provides temporary storage for data and program instructions being actively used by the CPU.
- ROM: Read-Only Memory, a type of computer memory that stores firmware or software instructions permanently and cannot be easily modified by the user.

- USB Type-C: A universal serial bus connector standard that features a reversible design, allowing for easier and more convenient connection of devices.

Specifications Summary

Here's a summary of the expected specifications for the OnePlus 12:

- Display: AMOLED display with high refresh rate and HDR support
- Processor: High-performance CPU (likely Qualcomm Snapdragon series)
- RAM: Generous RAM capacity for smooth multitasking

- Storage: Multiple storage options, with ample capacity for apps, media, and files
- Camera: Advanced camera system with multiple lenses, AI-powered features, and enhanced software capabilities
- Battery: Large battery capacity with fast charging support
- Connectivity: 5G connectivity, Wi-Fi, Bluetooth, NFC, and other standard connectivity options
- Software: OxygenOS based on the latest Android version, with customizable features and optimizations

Index

For quick reference, here's an index of topics covered in the OnePlus 12 review and user guide:

- Introduction to OnePlus 12
- Evolution of OnePlus Phones
- Anticipation and Expectations for OnePlus 12
- Unboxing and Initial Setup
- Design and Build Quality
- Display Technology
- Performance and Hardware
- Software and User Interface
- Camera System
- Battery Life and Charging
- Connectivity Options
- Audio Experience

- Security and Privacy Features
- Accessories and Additional Features
- Customization Tips
- Camera Tips and Tricks
- Troubleshooting and FAQs
- Conclusion

This index will help users easily navigate through the content and find information relevant to their needs and interests.